BETRAYAL

Warren Ravenscroft

Betrayal © Warren Ravenscroft 2024

ISBN: 978-0-6486422-9-9 (paperback)

The Chronological Study Bible
Copyright © 2008 by Thomas Nelson, Inc.

Scripture taken from the Spirit Filled Life Bible New King James Version®, Copyright ©1991 by Thomas Nelson, Inc.
Used by permission. All rights reserved.

All rights reserved. No part of this publication may be reproduced, stored in a retrieval system, or transmitted in any form or by any means electronic, mechanical, photocopying, recording, or otherwise, without the prior written permission of the author.

Published in Australia by Warren Ravenscroft.
www.wittonbooks.com

 A catalogue record for this book is available from the National Library of Australia

*"I will give you a new heart
and put a new spirit within you;
I will take the heart of stone
out of your flesh
and give you a heart of flesh."*

Ezekiel 36:26

Contents

Introduction	1
Abel. Prophet and Priest	5
The Life of Noah	35
Job's Righteous Journey	51
Joseph's Journey	71
Gideon. Mighty Man of Valour	103
Samson. Man of Power and Weakness	121
Prayers in the Old Testament	149
People Who Prayed in the Old Testament	171
The Angel of Lord Appearances	190
David's Life of Prayer	193
Prayers in the Old Testament. Final Thoughts	250
Betrayal	253
Judas the Betrayer	300
Other Books by the Author	314

Charts

Ancestry	4
People Who Prayed in the Old Testament	189
The Angel of the Lord Appearances	191
David's Prayer Psalms	248
Similarities between David and Jesus	249
Days and Events in the Easter Season	273
Trials and Outcome of Jesus	298

Introduction.

'Betrayal' is the loss of trust in others and yourself. It was Martin Luther who said, "Each betrayal begins with trust."

The saddest thing about betrayal is that it never comes from your enemies, it comes from those we trust the most.

The person most hurt by betrayal is the one who does it. Those closest to us can do the most damage. You can never really trust anyone, because no one is always loyal.

David understood betrayal. He wrote;

"For it is not an enemy who reproaches me;
then I could bear it.
Nor is it one who hates me
who has exalted himself against me;
then I could hide from him.
But it was you, a man my equal,
my companion and my acquaintance."

Psalm 55:12-13

Betrayal

Betrayal can only occur when there is love and trust. In the act of love, we let people into the most intimate aspect of our hearts, letting down our walls and protections. That's when we risk hurt and betrayal but that's also the place where true love dwells.

Peter and Judas were two who betrayed Jesus. Peter was given sufficient warning by Jesus about his pending actions, but Peter denied he would betray Jesus. Only a short time had passed before the rooster crowed, and Peter had betrayed Jesus three times.

Jesus, at the Lake of Tiberius, questioned Peter as to whether his love for Him was deep or surface. Jesus asked Peter if his love for Him was *'Agape'* (from the deepest part of his being), but Peter answered, *'Phileo'*, meaning He was just a friend.

Judas, on the other hand, betrayed Jesus out of selfish motives. One of the most common reasons is self-interest. People may betray others to gain power, money, or attention. The betrayer places their own needs above the well-being of others. Judas eventually realised he would rather die than live because he betrayed Jesus with the wrong motives in his heart.

Introduction.

Each Bible character featured in this book was betrayed in some way. They all had a form of trust and love for the person or persons who hurt them the most.

While some died as a consequence, others rose above the bitterness and hurt afforded to them, sometimes in the most unusual circumstances.

As you read and meditate on each person and the part life has given them to play, may you find encouragement that God has all in control, no matter how dark the way appears. May the following words bring comfort to those who have been betrayed.

> *"For His anger is but for a moment,*
> *His favour is for life;*
> *weeping may endure for a night,*
> *but joy comes in the morning."*
>
> Psalm 30:5

Ancestry

Adam and Eve had three sons

Cain   Able   Seth

9 Generations

Noah had three sons

Japheth   Shem   Ham

10 Generations

Abraham had eight sons

Hagar   Sarah   Keturah
(Maid Servant)   (Wife)   (Wife)

Isaac

Esau   Jacob had twelve sons

                            Joseph   Dan

        Manasseh   Ephraim   Manoah

Judah   Samson

10 Generations

David

42 Generations

Jesus

Abel. Prophet and Priest.

The following verses grabbed my attention.

"The wisdom of God said,
'I will send them prophets and apostles,
and some of them they will kill and persecute,
that the blood of all the prophets
which was shed from the foundation of the world
may be required of this generation,
from the blood of Abel to the blood of Zechariah
who perished between the altar and the temple'."

Luke 11:49-51a

"From the blood of Abel to the blood of Zechariah."
I had never noticed that Abel was a Prophet.

Jesus is in the last months of His earthly ministry, December to February, and it is winter time. Jesus had previously been challenged by a lawyer (Scribe), as to what he should do to inherit eternal life (Luke 10:25-37). A little later, Jesus is asked by a Pharisee to eat with invited Pharisees and Scribes so, Jesus seizes the moment and condemns them all under a section of "Woe's" (Luke 11:37-54). Jesus told them how they, and all the previous religious leaders were responsible for having killed the prophets God had sent.

Several questions were presented to me regarding this statement so, I looked up the reference to Zechariah and found it was 2 Chronicles 24:20-22. A second question was, "Why Abel and Zechariah were mentioned and not any of the other prophets?" How many others were there?

While I didn't follow through on the number, I did look at when the second book of Chronicles was written. My Bible told me, that it was between 425 and 400 B.C. This was the last written book of the Old Testament and attributed to Ezra. You would recall that after this book was written, four hundred years of silence reigned from God. I had always thought this book was written about the same time as Judges, and Kings.

If you choose to use our alphabet, it's A to Z or Abel to Zechariah. Jesus was the Alpha and Omega, First and Last. Jesus was saying that from the first prophet Abel in Eden, not the Garden of Eden, to the last Prophet Zechariah, the Jews and all their predecessors had been responsible for the Prophets' deaths. This raised the question, "Why did Jesus say that Abel was a prophet?" Let us define the word 'Prophet'.

"A Prophet conveyed the message of God,
sometimes with words, sometimes with actions,
sometimes with both and sometimes
merely the events of their lives served as prophecy."

We have no record of the things Abel said, however, his actions spoke louder than words.

Very little is known about Abel's life preceding the sacrifice he made to Father God. Adam and Eve had been expelled from the Garden of Eden, but not before the shedding of blood for the covering they would wear. This also covered their sin of disobedience and they were once again right with God.

When children were born, one would imagine that Adam and Eve told them what God had done in the Garden of Eden. God did not abandon Adam and Eve, as they would be like us. God would give them thoughts and direct speech to guide them in the way they had chosen to live.

Adam farmed the ground for a living as God had commanded (Genesis 3:17b). While the boys were growing in age, one could imagine that Adam also chose to be a shepherd and raise sheep. Diverse farming, I think it is called. Eventually, both boys would choose to follow in their fathers' footsteps. Cain, the eldest chose farming while Abel chose the life of a shepherd. One would also imagine that the others living in their community would have advised them how to farm and raise sheep. God never left His chosen family to their own devices.

We don't know a lot about Adam's family or what they were taught. Teaching should have been done by the parents, and God would have instructed them in the way they should act according to Him and His requirements. We are not told if Adam continued to sacrifice. What they were to observe concerning their living with the others who were created by God, not formed.

But there came a day when Cain instigated a sacrifice to Father God (Genesis 4:3). Hindsight shows us that he had the heart of his mother whereas Abel had the heart of his father. To understand the animosity between the two boys, we can use David and his brothers for an example (1 Samuel 17:28). The workers and the shepherd.

One could imagine Cain was ecstatic about his crops and fruit as he looked over the places he had cleared, tilled then planted seed. *'Look at what I have achieved'*, he may have thought.

He had forgotten that while he did the initial work, it was God who watered (Genesis 2:6) and God who bought the increase, and besides, the ground had been cursed by God. Genesis 3:17b

Satan offered Cain the same three temptations presented to his mother. The lust of the flesh, the lust of the eyes, and the pride of life. With this attitude, he approached Father God and presented his offering.

Abel also came to Father God, but the heart of Abel was different. He looked after the sheep, his small flock like his father tended the garden, led them to water and found good feeding areas. He cared for them day and night as he protected them from strangers. One could imagine he talked to them and called them by name. He had a relationship with each lamb or sheep. Although it was an ongoing process, a struggle, he cared and provided everything for them.

Many years later we are taught how Father God viewed this situation when Samuel was looking for the next king of Israel to anoint.

> *"For the Lord does not see as man sees;*
> *for man looks at the outward appearance,*
> *but the Lord looks at the heart."*
>
> 1 Samuel 16:7b

David wrote;

> *"The sacrifices of God are a broken spirit,*
> *a broken and a contrite heart.*
> *These, O God, You will not despise."*

Psalm 51:17

After Cain's offering had been rejected, God gave him a warning.

> *"If you do well, will you not be accepted?*
> *And if you do not well, sin lies at the door.*
> *And its desire is for you,*
> *but you should rule over it."*

Genesis 4:7

The Silent Prophet

Cain's heart was full of pride and we know that 'Pride comes before a fall'. As I previously mentioned, Cain was presented with three thoughts that were temptations similar in principle to what had been those given to his mother, Eve. Satan and his angels have never changed their tactics to deceive people as every temptation falls into one of the three categories, with no exceptions.

So, how did they apply to Cain and his thinking? The *'lust of the flesh'* is all about me, focusing on himself and ignoring God. Self-preservation as the older brother. The *'lust of the eyes'* is the expectation, exalting his own achievements of what he had achieved. The *'pride of life'* is not giving thanks to God for what He has accomplished. Cain's act was hollow as it was all about Cain and his achievements.

Abel was gentle and lowly because he understood what it was like to put the sheep and lambs before himself. Their well-being was of the utmost importance. Self-sacrifice was not an option. It would not have been easy for Abel to slaughter some of the firstborn lambs, and then bring their carcases to the altar along with the fat to be burnt. The fat would show how fit and acceptable the lambs were to be offered to Father God. You would remember that the Prodigal's father said to the servant, *"Kill the fatted calf."* Luke 15:23

Expecting a particular outcome, then finding that things don't go in your favour, brings resentment. Cain's reaction was all over his face as the word of God says, *"His countenance fell"* (Genesis 4:5b). The Lord noticed, and warned Cain that sin lay at his door, that sin desired to have him, but he should rule over it (v7), but Cain refused to acknowledge God's warning.

God's sacrifice of animals in the Garden established that a blood sacrifice was necessary when approaching Him. Right standing before a covenant-making God was shown to be a matter of life and death, not merely a matter of one's good deeds and efforts.

One could imagine Abel went back to his sheep in the field, to tend and care for them. Cain deliberately went to the field and found his younger brother and in anger, killed him. As the ground soaked up the blood of Abel, he died. It would be good to retrace our steps to obtain more understanding as to what transpired previously.

The difference between the brothers appeared to be in how each approached Father God. Because of their parent's sin, and gaining the knowledge of good and evil, Abel understood what God had done in the Garden so his parents could continue to have access to and fellowship with Him. Abel approached God in the same way by believing in faith whereas Cain dismissed the teaching.

As Cain instigated the sacrifices, was this a competition to prove little brother's thinking was wrong? One could accept that Cain saw everything had life in it as he watched his plants, trees and fields grow and bloom. Cain did virtually nothing after the initial preparation and planting of seeds as his job was over except for the occasional weed.

Abel saw life differently through the lives of his lambs and sheep as he was committed to them all day, seven days a week, providing for their care. He had a relationship with those he cared for. Cain was obsessed with proving little brother wrong. How do I know? Sibling rivalry.

Cain's expectations were high as he was the older brother. And so, the scene was set. Each would bring an offering and present what they thought was acceptable to Father God and He would show them, once and for all, the truth.

Did God send fire to consume Abel's sacrifice which changed the countenance of Cain? We are not told. With expectation came a consequence, so similar to Eve in the Garden. Cain had been deceived with his thinking as to how God should be approached. Humiliated in front of Abel, he became angry.

Father God then challenged Cain with the words;

> *"If you do well, will you not be accepted?*
> *And if you do not well, sin lies at the door.*
> *And its desire is for you,*
> *but you should rule over it."*

Genesis 4:7

God's reply to Cain told him to rethink his approach, but Cain refused to understand God. He went to the field where Abel was tending his flock and confronted him.

One could understand that Abel cared about Cain as he did for the flock in his care. As Abel tried to explain that the only way to approach Father God is through shed blood, this would have been like rubbing salt into a fresh wound. Cain's temper reached new heights and the sin that was at his door had the victory. How often do you share with someone but they don't listen to learn, they only listen to reply?

Abel was a prophet because he lived God's way. Although it is not recorded what he said to his brother, he spoke the words of God. Because Abel accepted God's way of approaching Him, he was right with God. His life and the words he spoke were God-given. Because of the blood sacrifice Abel made, he was made righteous before Father God. As Adam's attempt to use fig leaves for a covering was rejected, so was Cairn's offering.

Our approach to Father God can only be attained through faith. The writer to the Hebrews gave the following sound advice;

> *"Without faith it is impossible to please Him,*
> *for he who comes to God must believe that He is,*
> *and that He is a rewarder*
> *of those who diligently seek Him."*
>
> Hebrews 11:6

Abel still teaches us today, because of his approach to Father God, that the only way to God must be through shed blood. When we approach God, it is through Jesus who made the perfect sacrifice for us. Through faith in what Jesus did, we have access to God.

Three verses of scripture support this view.

> *"There is a way that seems right to a man,*
> *but its end is the way of death."*
>
> Proverbs 14:12

> *"For by grace you have been saved through faith,*
> *and not of yourselves, it is the gift of God,*
> *not of works, lest anyone should boast."*
>
> Ephesians 2:8-9

> *"If you confess with your mouth*
> *the Lord Jesus and believe in your heart*
> *that God has raised Him from the dead,*
> *you will be saved.*
> *For with the heart one believes unto righteousness,*
> *and with the mouth*
> *confession is made unto salvation."*
>
> Romans 10:9-10

The Silent Priest

I had never contemplated that the original verse of scripture (Luke 11:49-51a) would lead me on such a diverse path. The more I delved into the text, the more the Holy Spirit revealed there was to research. One night in frustration, I prayed to the Lord, and presented my plea to Him, asking Him that while He had given me wisdom, would He please give me understanding?

In the early hours of the morning, around 2 am, I was woken from sleep. I was wide awake. I said to the Lord, "What do you want to tell me?" For the next two and a half hours, we shared, me writing down each thought as it came. In the morning, I shared with Bev that the Lord had woken me during the night. She said to me, "What did He say?" I said, "Where do I begin?"

As I reread the account in Genesis, I realised everyone created or formed were vegetarians as people did not eat meat. Let me share with you the following verses.

"And God said,
'See, I have given you every herb that yields seed
which is on the face of all the earth,
and every tree whose fruit yields seed;
to you it shall be for food.
Also, to every beast of the earth,

Abel. Prophet and Priest.

> *to every bird of the air,*
> *and to everything that creeps on the earth,*
> *in which there is life,*
> *I have given every green herb for food',*
> *and it was so."*

Genesis 1:29-30

This became clearer when I read the following.

> *"Cursed is the ground for your sake;*
> *in toil you shall eat of it all the days of your life.*
> *Both thorns and thistles it shall bring forth for you,*
> *and you shall eat the herb of the field."*

Genesis 3:17b-18

Adam's life and all those who lived and ate of the ground were suddenly thrown into an unfamiliar realm of chaos. They were required to work the ground to obtain food. Were they ready for the unexpected? Adam and Eve would always remember their time spent in the Garden of Eden.

Later, God gave instructions to Noah about the food for his family and the animals. God said;

Betrayal

> *"And you shall take for yourself*
> *of all food that is eaten,*
> *and you shall gather it to yourself;*
> *and it shall be food for you and for them."*
>
> Genesis 6:21

Herbs of the field for Noah, his family and the animals.

After the flood, God said to Noah;

> *"The fear of you and the dread of you*
> *shall be on every beast of the earth,*
> *on every bird of the air,*
> *on all that move on the earth,*
> *and on the fish of the sea.*
> *They are given into your hand.*
> *Every moving thing that lives shall be food for you.*
> *I have given you all things,*
> *even as the green herbs."*
>
> Genesis 9:2-3

Verse four placed the only restriction on future generations that drinking the blood was forbidden.

So, I ask the question, "Why was Abel a shepherd if they didn't eat meat?" (Genesis 4:2). I thought about sheep, wool for clothing, milk and cheese and other products of the day that could have been used to supplement all the herbs, fruit and grains. Adam and Eve should have taught their sons about the blood sacrifice required to cover their sins.

Abel understood that a blood sacrifice was required to approach God, and he became the first person to offer a blood sacrifice. Abel was the first priest as he not only talked the talk, but he walked the walk. In other words, he spoke to Father God and carried out His instructions. The Lord had carried out the killing of the animals for Adam and Eve to cover their sin so, Abel was selected to slaughter the firstborn lambs and sacrifice them to God as a righteous offering. Animals were for sacrifice, but they were not to be eaten.

When *the Lord said to Cain, "Where is Abel your brother?"* Cain lied, for he said, *"I do not know."* He then said, *"Am I my brother's keeper?"* (Genesis 4:9), shifting the focus. Didn't his parents do the same thing in the Garden of Eden? He hadn't learnt much. *The Lord replied, "What have you done? The voice of your brother's blood cries out to Me from the ground"* (v10). The reason that Abel's blood cried out to the Lord was that he was the first righteous person to die.

Abel's priestly offering had covered any sin committed, so he was found without blame in the sight of Father God. God accepted Abel's gift because he gave it in faith. The Lord passed swift judgment on Cain as he had not learnt anything from his parents and the consequences that accompanied such wilful disobedience.

When Cain killed Abel, who was available to offer a sacrifice for Cain's sin? God dealt severely with Cain and sent him away, but Cain pleaded with the Lord, as the punishment was more than he could bear, so God put a mark on him for protection. The grace of God came into place, even though Cain's sin was not forgiven (Genesis 4:11-15). Cain left the presence of the Lord and dwelt with the others God had created in the land of Nod on the east of Eden.

Time passed and Seth was born to Adam and Eve. With the passing of years, men began to call on the name of the Lord once again (Genesis 4:26). One could imagine that the way of animal sacrifice had been reinstated for the forgiveness of sin, and a pleasing aroma from the burnt sacrifices made, reached heaven and pleased Father God.

Before we continue, we need to ask the question, "Is this relevant to me?" I want to suggest that Cain killed Abel for three reasons.

Abel. Prophet and Priest.

1. Abel's righteous status before and concerning God. Matthew 23:35
2. Cain envied Abel's faith. Hebrews 11:1–4
3. Abel was resented for his prophetic office. Luke 11:49–51

Is there anyone whom you admire or envy concerning their standing with God? Do you admire or envy the faith or trust a person appears to possess? Are you envious that others receive recognition and you appear to be thrust aside?

Sometimes obedience to Father God comes with a high price. Abel's example teaches us today that even though he died for truth, he did not die in vain. His life still speaks. It reminds us to count the cost of obedience. Are we willing to follow and obey God, no matter how great the sacrifice is?

Do we trust God even if it costs our very lives? I once read, "Leave an inheritance that lives on after you have gone to your eternal reward." What will you be remembered for? What will I be remembered for? The Bible reminds us that;

> *"In all things*
> *He may have the pre-eminence."*
>
> Colossians 1:18b

Abel. A Foreshadow of Jesus.

Many years would pass before Moses would write what Abel understood about life in the blood.

> *"For the life of the flesh is in the blood,*
> *and I have given it to you upon the altar*
> *to make atonement for your souls;*
> *for it is the blood*
> *that makes atonement for the soul."*
>
> Leviticus 17:11

Ever since God chose for Himself a people, they have been persecuted, almost to the point of extinction. But although many have tried, they are still protected and survive to this day. First was the Egyptian Empire. The Assyrian Empire followed. The Babylonian Empire also tried as did the Persian Empire. The Greek Empire was followed by the Roman Empire which saw the dispersion of the Jewish race worldwide.

While other persecution existed, it was Hitler during the Second World War, who tried unsuccessfully to eradicate the entire Jewish race. While all the previous Empires have vanished from history, the Jewish race survived until the present day and will continue to do so.

One could ask the question, "Did no one learn from past events?" Presently Hamas is persecuting the Jewish race. As history unfolds, they too will disappear from the world scene. All who came against God's chosen people have come to nothing.

As we have considered the various aspects of Cain and Abel's lives, Abel foreshadowed Jesus. A careful study will reveal the following.

- Abel was a shepherd. Genesis 4:2
- Our Lord is a Shepherd. 'The Good Shepherd'. John 10:11
- It was as a shepherd, that Abel presented his offering unto God. Genesis 4:4
- It was as a Shepherd that Jesus Christ presented His offering to God. John 10:11
- Though giving no cause for it, Abel was hated by his brother. Genesis 4:8
- Jesus, though giving no cause for it, was hated by His brethren according to the flesh of the Jews. John 15:25
- Cain was jealous of his brother Abel and it was out of envy that Cain slew Abel. Genesis 4:7
- It was through the Pharisees' envy that Jesus was delivered up to be crucified. Matthew 27:18
- Abel did not die a natural death. Genesis 4:8

- Our Lord did not die a natural death. He was slain by 'wicked hands'. Acts 2:23
- Abel met a violent end at the hand of his brother. Genesis 4:8
- Jesus was crucified by 'the house of Israel', His brethren according to the flesh. Romans 9:5
- Punishment was meted out upon Abel's murderer. Genesis 4:11-12
- After His death, our Lord's murderers were punished by God. Mark 12:9
- The offering Abel presented was an offering *"unto God."* Hebrews 11:4
- The Lord Jesus was presented as an offering *"to God."* Ephesians 5:2
- The offering that Abel presented was *"the firstlings of his flock"*, a *"lamb."* Genesis 4:4
- The offering Jesus presented was Himself; a *"lamb."* 2 Peter 1:19
- In bringing his offering *"by faith"* Abel demonstrated that he believed the Word of God. Hebrews 11:4
- In presenting Himself as an offering Jesus was obedient to *"the Word of God."* Hebrews 10:7-9
- The offering that Abel presented is described as an *"excellent"* one. Hebrews 11:4
- The offering Christ offered was an *"excellent"* one. It was *"a sweet-smelling savour."* Ephesians 5:2

- God had *"respect unto Abel and to his offering."* God accepted the offering of Abel. Hebrews 11:4
- God accepted Jesus' offering. The proof is that He is now *"seated at the right hand of God."* Hebrews 10:12
- In the presentation of his offering, Abel *"obtained witness that he was righteous."* Hebrews 11: 4
  Abel was already saved and made righteous.
- While presenting Himself on the Cross as an offering to God, *"He obtained witness that He was righteous."* The centurion said, *"This is a righteous man."* Luke 23:47
- After Abel presented his offering, God publicly *"testified"* of His acceptance of it. Hebrews 11:4
- God publicly testified His acceptance of the offering by raising Jesus from the dead. Acts 2:36
- Abel's offering still *"speaks"* to God. By it, Abel *"being dead yet speaketh."* Hebrews 11:4
- Christ's offering now *"speaks"* to God. Hebrews 12:24

As the above comparison leaves us without a doubt, Abel was a foreshadowing of Jesus, although he was unaware. It is only because we have hindsight, that we can understand. Understanding is given to us by the Holy Spirit. But there is one other observation I would share with you. It has all to do with the *'Altars'*.

Cain instigated the sacrifices. He was proud of what he had achieved with his crops, herbs, vegetables and various fruits. One could imagine the two brothers standing before the barren, stark, stone altars. Cain dressed and adorned his altar with the produce. It would have looked pleasing to the eyes—such beauty to behold.

Then Abel could have adorned his altar. The blood dripped from the slaughter of his lamb, the fat also being removed and placed beside the sacrifice, as the blood continued to flow into the stones and be swallowed up. This would have repulsed the onlooker when compared to the beauty of Cains' altar.

I could imagine, as both brothers stood near their altars, eagerly awaiting God's approval, fire descended and consumed Abel's sacrifice, and Cain's countenance fell. Cain's offering represented the cursed ground. This represents what the world has to offer and is embraced by so many. Abel's offering represented the way of the cross, for we are told;

> *"He was despised and rejected by men,*
> *a Man of sorrows and acquainted with grief.*
> *And we hid, as it were,*
> *our faces from Him.*
> *He was despised*
> *and we did not esteem Him."*
>
> Isaiah 53:3

As I continued to think about the altars, I thought of the three crosses that represented three altars on Calvary. On the middle altar was Jesus laying Himself down obediently to obey His Father's will. On either side were two other altars. What was being offered on each of these?

We hear the words from one thief, *"If you are the Christ, save yourself and us"* (Luke 23:37). The thief was thinking about himself as people do today. It's all about self-preservation, all about me and what I want. This is similar to the altar of Cain. On the other side, we hear the reply of the other thief, *"Do you not even fear God, seeing you are under the same condemnation?"*

"We indeed justly, for we receive the due reward of our deeds, but this Man has done nothing wrong. Lord, remember me when You come into Your kingdom" (v40-42). This is like the altar of Abel, an acceptable sacrifice to Father God. And Jesus said to him;

> *"Assuredly, I say to you,*
> *today you will be with Me in Paradise."*
>
> Luke 23:43

Jesus, with arms outstretched, bleeding, as His blood trickled down His body and onto the ground which soaked up the drops of blood. As His side was pierced, out flowed blood and water to be soaked up by the earth, and the centurion confessed, *"Truly, this was the Son of God!"* Matthew 27:54b

Jesus was killed on an altar between two other altars. One was of the world, thinking of himself, the other seeking forgiveness. A Cain altar and an Abel altar. Because of the perfect sacrifice offered and accepted by Father God, Jesus sat at the right hand of His Father. The seeking thief was found righteous because of what Jesus had accomplished only minutes before the inquiring thief's death.

Mary Jones (1810-1883), wrote the following words I would share with you.

My body, soul and spirit, Jesus, I give to Thee,
a consecrated offering, Thine evermore to be.

O Jesus, mighty Saviour, I trust in Thy great name.
I look for Thy salvation, Thy promise now I claim.

O let the fire, descending just now upon my soul,
consume my humble offering, and cleanse and make me whole.

My all is on the altar, I'm waiting for the fire.
Waiting, waiting, waiting,
I'm waiting for the fire.

Public Domain

We each have an altar on which our life's work will be placed. Is this relevant to me? Words of scripture help bring the efforts we do in this life, into focus. Paul, when writing to the Corinthians wrote;

"Now if anyone builds on this foundation with
gold, silver, precious stones, wood, hay, straw,
each one's work will become clear;
for the Day will declare it,
because it will be revealed by fire;
and the fire will test each one's work,
of what sort it is.
If anyone's work which he has built on it endures,
he will receive a reward.
If anyone's work is burned,
he will suffer loss;
but he himself will be saved,
yet so as through fire."

1 Corinthians 3:12-15

We have travelled together the story of Abel, as the Holy Spirit has spoken to each one's soul. We all have an altar on which we place our offerings to Father God, daily as we live our lives. The question that is in my mind is, "Does God accept all our offerings, all that is presented to Him?" There are two guidelines to answer this question.

1. Was the offering offered in 'Faith'?
2. Did what we do bring glory to Father God or us?

For many years I completed much out of duty, believing it was my reasonable service. I completed the tasks because it was what was expected. I guess, as I reflect, it was more for the praise of man than for the glory of God, that much was completed.

Jesus' reflection about sheep and goats has weighed heavily on my heart for many years. My Bible says, *"By their fruits you will know them"* (Matthew 7:20). I was concerned about the number of 'supposedly' saved people who committed their life to works. It was all about them and what they accomplished. It was about the acclaim of man and how they had blessed people with their works. There was no mention of glory to God. How could these converts be deceived to the stage that work was enough? I was looking for the fruit produced.

Fresh enlightenment came when I read the preceding verse from Corinthians. When each of us approaches the throne of

God and lays our life's offering on the altar, fire descends and burns up all the wood, hay and straw, but will there be any gold, silver or precious stones remaining? 1 Corinthians 3:12

While I would choose to think that all things precious will be found, the reality is that my account, recorded in the Book of Life, could be somewhat different and show a deficit. Because of the word of God, I can take heart. Paul when writing to the Corinthians said;

> *"If anyone's work is burned,*
> *he will suffer loss;*
> *but he himself will be saved,*
> *yet so as through fire."*

The assurance of entrance into heaven brings a wonderful sense of thankfulness. But Peter adds further to what will happen at the judgement when he wrote his first epistle.

> *"That the genuineness of your faith,*
> *being much more precious than gold that perishes,*
> *though it is tested by fire,*
> *may be found to praise, honour,*
> *and glory at the revelation of Jesus Christ,*
> *whom having not seen you love."*
>
> 1 Peter 1:7-8a

Even our best efforts of pleasing Father God will be tested for acceptability. The gold, silver and precious jewels, may all suffer loss, but genuine faith is required to enter into eternity. What is placed on our altar has nothing to do with any works we have completed, no matter how acceptable they proved to be. What will matter most is if we were set apart for the kingdom's sake, holy acceptable to Father God, always ready to do His will.

While I may not have much left to say thank you to Jesus for what He did for me, to receive any crowns, I am assured, having accepted Jesus as my Lord and Saviour through faith, that I will be permitted to spend eternity with Him.

Paul was writing to the Christians at Corinth, not to those outside the then-known church. This was all about the saved, not the unsaved. The Judgement on man had been carried out. Most had their incorruptible body and soul destroyed and been assigned to burn in the lake of fire for eternity. Matthew 10:28

The others, who know the saving power of the shed blood of Jesus, are now being judged for the works they completed for God. Once the fire has cleansed our works, what is left will be given to us as crowns or rewards, to lay down at the feet of Jesus as a thank offering.

The goats are those who blatantly refuse to accept Jesus as their Lord and Saviour. This also includes those who see that living a good life, will be enough. Also, those who regularly attend church and love hearing about Jesus and doing many works, and supporting, but never come to an understanding. Paul addressed this type of person when writing to Timothy said, *"Always learning and never able to come to the knowledge of the truth."* 2 Timothy 3:7

The sheep are those who have heard the voice of the Shepherd and have given themselves completely in obedience and continue to serve Him as the Spirit leads. This is where what we present as our sacrifice is important. The difference is, does it bring glory to God or us? Our sacrificial life is not about works that adorn us, but what is pleasing to Father God. It has been said, "It's not in the doing but all in the being."

I remember being part of a combination. We rehearsed and practised for months to perfect our music. We were to leave late Friday night and fly to New Zealand where we would play to many people over the coming weeks. At the end of the final rehearsal, the chaplain asked one of the members to pray. The prayer went like this. *Father God. We have finished our last rehearsal. We have played our last note. We as a band place our offering on Your altar as our sacrifice to You. May what we present to Your people be acceptable to You and bring You the glory.*

While there were many fun times and much applause, there did not appear to be any visible movement of people's souls. On another occasion, the months before embarking on an extensive Eastern Australian tour, everything was bathed in prayer. Souls were saved, and the visible presence of the Holy Spirit was always present. Was one a Cain offering and the other an Abel? Only on judgement day will we know for sure if God owned and blessed our offerings.

Let me share a verse of scripture with you.

May the words of my mouth and the meditations of my heart,
be acceptable to You,
my Lord my Rock and my Redeemer.

Psalm 19:14

The Life of Noah.

When we hear the name 'Noah', usually our thoughts turn to his association with the Ark or boat, God had instructed him to build. But there is so much more to be gained from this simple children's story for those who would study to find themselves approved by God.

Ancestry.

Noah was a distant relative of Adam and Eve. Adam had a son Seth, who had a son Enosh, who had a son Cainan, who had a son Mahalalel, who had a son Jared, who had a son Enoch, who had a son Methuselah, who had a son Lamech, who had a son Noah, who had three sons, Shem, Ham and Japheth.

The Pending Storm.

Noah is recorded as *'a just man, perfect in his generations. Noah walked with God'* (Genesis 6:9). When God looked upon the earth He had created, He saw corruption and violence. God knew that Noah was righteous in all his ways because he walked with God. The two had a relationship that was sadly lacking between God and all the other inhabitants.

God told Noah, because he found grace in the sight of God, what He planned for mankind, and it was not good. God outlined His plan for Noah to build an Ark. He gave him the plans and Noah obediently carried out the revealed will of God.

Noah didn't listen to other people who questioned his actions. He obeyed God. He started building a boat and preaching the message of righteousness. He told people it was going to rain because God had said so. People dismissed what Noah was saying as no one could comprehend what he meant by rain. Before the flood, it had never rained downwards from the heavens, but rather water vapour lifted up from the earth.

> *"A mist went up from the earth*
> *and watered the whole face of the ground."*
>
> Genesis 2:6

The Bible does not specify how long the ark took to construct, although one hundred and twenty years have been suggested by scholars in the past. Noah was likely mocked for building a giant boat when no flood was yet seen upon the earth, but he did not worry about what other people thought. He simply responded to God's commands with a willing heart and hands. God rewarded him for his righteousness and obedience, saving both Noah and his family from destruction.

Noah was obedient and blameless in the eyes of God, which allowed him to develop two fundamental characteristics, 'Faith' and 'Patience'. The apostle James reminds us that *"the testing of your faith produces patience"* (James 1:3). Noah was called to persevere and trust in God's plan for him and his family.

The day came when God told Noah to take his wife, along with his sons and their wives and go inside the Ark. God gave specific instructions as to what animals and how many were to be allowed on board.

> *"You shall take with you seven each of every clean animal,*
> *a male and his female;*
> *two each of animals that are unclean,*
> *a male and his female;*
> *also seven each of birds of the air,*
> *male and female,*
> *to keep the species alive on the face of all the earth."*
>
> Genesis 7:2-3

One could only wonder if Noah had the support of his wife and family? Did they encourage him or discourage him during the construction years? When he encouraged them to go into the Ark, did they go willingly? Did they view this as something to do to appease the old man? We are not told. What we are told is that they went into the Ark and the selected animals went in also, under God's direction.

What did they think walking around the levels of the Ark, looking at all the contented animals? All thoughts of returning to their residences were suddenly, and without warning dismissed as;

> "The Lord shut them in."
>
> Genesis 7:16b

The screams of people outside the closed door as the rain descended and the flood waters began to rise, would not have been easy to endure. Their friends, and other members of the son's wives' families, must have pleaded to be let in, but even if Noah and those inside wanted to, God had closed the door. The time to accept the invitation was past.

Eventually, everything went quiet except for the rain that continued for forty days and nights. As the Ark lifted and moved, nothing could have prepared them for this, even Noah. The animals were quiet and relaxed as the family members moved around to feed them. There was no fighting, even amongst the most fearsome, because they all ate grass and grain, the same as Noah and his family. Everyone, including animals, were vegetarian before the flood.

Supplying food for about a year-long journey, would not be easy. I am reminded that this mission was ordained by God, not by man. God was well able to take care of everything, as He did at a later time when caring for the children of Israel.

> *"I led you forty years in the wilderness.*
> *Your clothes have not worn out,*
> *and your sandals have not worn out on your feet."*
>
> Deuteronomy 29:5

What God ordains, He supplies. Paul, when writing to the Philippians, reminded those of his congregation about God supplying all their need. Was this time any different to those of the future?

> *"And my God shall supply all your needs*
> *according to His riches in glory*
> *by Christ Jesus."*
>
> Philippians 4:19

The lowing of the contented beasts or the occasional call of a bird formed the background of the quietness that surrounded the occupants. The rain had stopped and an eeriness invaded the atmosphere which had to be heard to be appreciated. As the Ark swayed minimally, Noah and his family had no idea what was happening on the outside. But then the swaying stopped.

Noah took one of the ravens and set it free through the window in the top of the Ark. They could see the tops of the mountains, as the flood had receded, but the ground was still covered with water. He sent out a dove which eventually returned with an olive leaf in her mouth. After another seven days, the dove did not return, so;

> *"Noah removed the covering of the Ark and looked,*
> *and indeed the surface of the ground was dry."*
>
> Genesis 8:13b

The Ark had rested on Mount Ararat. God told Noah to vacate the Ark along with his family and animals.

> *"So Noah went out, and his sons*
> *and his wife and his son's wives with him.*
> *Every animal, every creeping thing,*
> *every bird, and whatever creeps on the earth,*
> *according to their families,*
> *went out of the ark."*
>
> Genesis 8:18

A new day dawned, and a new life for Noah and his family. How different to the old life they had known. Noah built an altar to the Lord and took of every clean animal and of every clean bird and offered burnt offerings on the altar. *The Lord smelled a soothing aroma, and said in His heart, "I will never again curse the ground for man's sake, although the imagination of man's heart is evil from his youth; nor will I again destroy everything as I have done."*

The Life of Noah.

God made a covenant with creation.

> *"While the earth remains,*
> *seedtime and harvest,*
> *cold and heat,*
> *winter and summer,*
> *and day and night*
> *shall not cease."*
>
> Genesis 8:22

God blessed Noah and his sons, and said;

> *"Be fruitful and multiply, and fill the earth.*
> *And the fear of you and the dread of you*
> *shall be on every beast of the earth,*
> *on every bird of the air,*
> *on all that moves on earth,*
> *and on all the fish of the sea.*
> *They are given into your hand.*
> *Every moving thing that lives*
> *shall be food for you."*
>
> Genesis 9:1-3a

The world they knew had changed. They were encouraged to eat meat, not just grain.

God made a second covenant with Noah and his sons, and their descendants after them. With every living creature that is with you: the birds, the cattle, and every beast of the earth with you, of all that go out of the ark, every beast of the earth. And God said;

> *"The rainbow shall be in the cloud,*
> *and I will look on it to remember*
> *the everlasting covenant*
> *between God and every living creature*
> *of all flesh that is on earth."*
>
> Genesis 9:16-17

A new era, a new beginning with eight people. What could possibly go wrong? So much wisdom, knowledge and understanding about the past to build on. God had provided for their safety and provision during the last year. God had addressed Noah and his sons and covenanted with them about the future days and their descendants, blessing them in ways they had not known, but their part was to do the revealed will of Father God.

Time passed for this small community. Children were born to families and life went on. Eventually, Noah planted a vineyard and reaped a harvest, as God brought blessings to them all. Noah's family may have all survived the flood, but they were born of man, meaning, the sinful nature was still within each of them.

Unexpectedly, Noah consumed too much of the wine he had produced and became drunk from the effects of the fermented wine. Although Noah was in the privacy of his tent, it was obvious to Ham that he was making a spectacle of himself. He went and watched his father and was amused at the behaviour of this righteous man, one who walked with God, acting this way.

Ham encouraged his two brothers, Shem and Japheth to watch their father in his drunken stupor, but they would not.

"They took a garment,
laid it on both their shoulders,
and went backwards
and covered the nakedness of their father.
Their faces turned away,
and they did not see their father's nakedness."

Genesis 9:23

One could imagine that Ham found pleasure in gossiping and spreading to everyone what he had seen, especially to his son, Canaan. When Noah awoke, he knew what his younger son had done. He prayed to Father God and said;

> *"Cursed be Canaan;*
> *a servant of servants*
> *he shall be to his brethren.*
> *Blessed be the Lord,*
> *the God of Shem,*
> *and may Canaan be his servant.*
> *May God enlarge Japhet,*
> *and may he dwell in the tents of Shem;*
> *and may Canaan be his servant."*
>
> Genesis 9:25-27

Noah lived three hundred and fifty years after the flood and was nine hundred and fifty years old when he died.

The families of the three sons, Japhet, Shem and Ham, grew and had children of their own, and their children had children until a great number filled their part of the earth. Many people and tribes were assembled together and they all spoke the native tongue of their fathers. There was one language and one speech. As the numbers grew, so they expanded their borders. They travelled east until they found a plain in the land of Shinar, and they dwelt there.

Pride has always been a sin since Satan was expelled from heaven. Pride infiltrated every culture and the thoughts of man, and these people did not escape the sin of pride. They had the knowledge to build a city for themselves, but that wasn't enough. They chose to build a tower that reached into the heavens, to not only make a name for themselves but to safeguard themselves from scattering all over the world.

Many years would pass before Solomon would pen the words;

> *"A man's heart plans his way,*
> *but the Lord directs his steps."*

Proverbs 16:9

When the tower was finished, but the city was incomplete, the Lord came to inspect what they had done. Realizing the people could do much more than they purposed, He said;

> *"Come, let Us go down*
> *and there confuse their language,*
> *that they may not understand*
> *one another's speech."*

Genesis 11:7

What these people feared most came upon them.

> *"The Lord scattered them abroad from there*
> *over the face of all the earth,*
> *and they ceased building the city,*
> *therefore its name is called Babel"*
>
> Genesis 11:8-9a

Noah's prayer had a long and lasting effect on the descendants of his three sons. While the descendants of Japhet and Shem were blessed, the descendants of Ham were cursed, they were all dispersed to many locations over the earth. Some of the tribes or clans named cities and areas after some of their predecessors, such as Canaan, Egypt, Cush, Babylon, Nineveh and Raamah to name but a few. This would have a great effect on the chosen people, the children of Israel, as they fought and conquered the promised land.

Everywhere the children of Israel went, who they fought against and killed, were distant relatives of Ham. The curse placed on Ham's son Canaan by Noah was to be carried out as directed by Father God. Just as Ham had no respect for his father, so these related people, so many generations on, would have no respect for the chosen of God, the people He had called to be His separated people.

The Significance of Noah's Story.

Noah's life has a prophetic meaning for all humanity. God rewarded Noah for his righteousness and obedience. The story of the Flood also demonstrates both the gravity of God's justice and the promise of His salvation. Every sin we commit grieves God, and His justice demands judgment for that sin.

Because Noah had persevered and trusted in God's plan for him, God made a covenant promise between Himself, Noah and His creation, symbolized by a rainbow. We need to choose to remain faithful to God instead of worrying about what other people think.

The Noah's Ark story gives us many lessons to apply to our lives today. It teaches us that God provides us with a way to begin again when we make mistakes. When we don't understand God's plan, we can trust Him to fill our lives with the blessings and resources that we need.

The Ark Noah built compared to Jesus.

God instructed Noah to build a doorway in the right-hand side of the ark, which he did. The doorway was the only entrance by which he, his family and the animals could access the inside of the ark. The only way to Father God is through His Son, Jesus Christ. Jesus Himself said;

> *"I am the Door.*
> *If anyone enters by Me,*
> *he will be saved,*
> *and will go in and out and find pasture."*

John 10:9

There is no reference to which side of Jesus was pierced by the centurion when blood and water flowed out. One would imagine the right side was pierced, as the spear was required to travel through the lungs and heart, releasing the water around both. The left side would not have achieved this outcome.

Jesus referred to the right when teaching about the sheep and goats (Matthew 25:31-46). The right hand is seen as a place of honour and status throughout the biblical text. Jesus Christ Himself sat down at the right hand of the Father. Hebrews 10:12b

Jesus also taught that;

> *"I am the way, the truth, and the life.*
> *No one comes to the Father*
> *except through Me."*

John 14:6

When Jesus looked over Jerusalem He lamented over their response to the many prophets and messengers whom the Father had sent, and how they had killed their message and many of them. One could imagine Jesus, lifting His right arm sideways and saying;

> *"How often I wanted to gather*
> *your children together,*
> *as a hen gathers her chicks under her wings,*
> *but you were not willing."*

Matthew 23:37b

Just as the ark had only one door as an entrance into the safety and protection of what was about to happen, so Jesus is the only way to the Father, providing shelter and protection for us here on earth before the day of judgement is thrust on each one.

The Ark of Noah compared to the Ark of the Covenant.

The story of the Ark includes three topics: Noah, the Provision of Food, and the Protection provided by the Ark.

The Ark of the Covenant contained three items. The tablets of the covenant, the golden pot containing manna, and Aaron's rod that budded. Hebrews 9:4

- The 'Tablets of stone' represented the 'Law of God'. Noah was righteous because he kept the law.
- Manna in the Jar was God's provision for the children of Israel in the desert. God's provision provided for those in the Ark.
- Aron's Rod that budded. The assurance of new life after release from the Ark.

We enter the Ark of God through the shed blood of Jesus and are found righteous before Father God. Because of what Jesus did, not by our works, God provides for our well-being between this life and the next. Being found faithful, we have the assurance of new life, living in the presence of Father God for eternity.

Noah's Ark is a representation of the Ark of the Covenant in Moses day. The spiritual presence of the Lord as a protector and guide for the Israelites in exchange for them keeping God's commandments. There is a long tradition in Christian thought of Noah as a type of Christ and his Ark as an allegory of salvation. Once the redeemed, the called have entered in through the Door, Jesus Christ, they are preserved in the Ark for time and eternity.

Job's Righteous Journey.

"Do not grumble against one another,
brethren, lest you be condemned.
Behold, the Judge is standing at the door!
My brethren, take the prophets,
who spoke in the name of the Lord,
as an example of suffering and patience.
Indeed we count them blessed who endure.
You have heard of the perseverance of Job
and seen the end intended by the Lord,
that the Lord is very compassionate and merciful."

James 5:9-11

Job's ancestry began with Abraham. Much has been written about Abraham and God dealing with him and his descendants. Abraham had a brother by the name of Nahor. In Genesis 22:20, Nahor married Milcah and gave birth to eight sons. The most notable of Milcah's sons was Kemuel, the father of Aram. Aram was a distant relation of Shem (Genesis 11:10-26) and had a son named Uz. Job was of the tribe of Uz.

Job was rich, prosperous and a blessed man because he was blameless and upright, and one who feared God and shunned evil (Job 1:1b). Job observed the sacrificial shedding of blood for remission of sins. He was a priest before Father God, as he regularly atoned for his children after their feast days, as he was aware they may have sinned and cursed God in their hearts. Job 1:5

The account of Job's struggles has been written to give us insight into the unseen satanic attack that can affect our daily life and all God has permitted us to be good stewards of. We do not need to know the intricacies of what is happening in the background but have faith and trust in God to know He has our best interests at heart as He will not let us be tempted beyond our capabilities. 1 Corinthians 10:13

The writer to the Hebrews in chapter eleven, mentions many selected for their faith in times of testing, but Job is not included in the list. However, James recorded that Job was remembered for his patience, not faith. This did not mean Job did not have faith, but along with patience, he persevered through faith, in trust, to reach the result God had predestined for him.

Father God had confidence in Job and suggested to Satan the following when Satan was found amongst the sons of God.

> *Then the Lord said to Satan,*
> *"Have you considered My servant Job,*
> *that there is none like him on the earth,*
> *a blameless and upright man,*
> *one who fears God and shuns evil."*
>
> Job 1:8

God had instigated the conversation with Satan because God was confident that Satan did not have complete rule over all His formed people. Satan came back with a counterattack challenging God to wreak havoc on Job to see how true he would remain. How blatant is Satan to challenge God? The subtleness of Satan, God understood as He had created him and knew his deceptive heart.

Paul, many years later, when writing to the Corinthian church says;

> *"For God is not the author of confusion*
> *but of peace."*
>
> 1 Corinthians 14:33a

God placed the ball back in Satan's court. Satan left God's presence, and Job was unaware of what was about to happen to him, his family, and his possessions. This was all about God and not about Job.

One could imagine Job waking to another day, not expecting anything out of the ordinary, but in the passing of a few hours, Job's whole life was turned around. Job lost all of his children, seven sons and three daughters, and his wealth in a single day. Job 1:13-19

One could imagine the emotions of loss would have been great, but Job remained blameless before the Lord and blessed His name in worship. *"In all this Job did not sin nor charge God with wrong."* Job 1:22

Satan was antagonistic to Father God and showed up a second time and God knew why he was there. God said to Satan;

> *Have you considered My servant Job,*
> *that there is none like him on the earth,*
> *a blameless and upright man,*
> *one who fears God and shuns evil?*
> *And still he holds fast to his integrity,*
> *although you incited Me against him,*
> *to destroy him without cause."*
>
> Job 2:3

God knew exactly what Satan was up to the first time he came into His presence. Satan doesn't change his tactic, because, for the second time, he tried to coerce God into doing what He couldn't do, and that was to bring confusion. Satan said, *"Stretch out Your hand now, and touch his bone and his flesh, and he will surely curse You to Your face!"* Job 2:5

God truly understands every temptation that He allows to be presented to us. The grace of God will cover every situation we encounter. God knew Job would be faithful and persevere so, the reply came permitting Satan, not God to act, for He said;

> *"Behold,*
> *he is in your hand,*
> *but spare his life."*
>
> Job 2:6

The grace of God supplied boundaries that Satan was allowed to operate in. *"So, Satan went out from the presence of the Lord."* Job 2:7a

Job was covered in painful boils, from the sole of his foot to the crown of his head. His wife offered him no support but encouraged him to give up, curse God, and die (Job 2:9). While she was probably mourning the loss of her children and lifestyle, she was of no support to Job in his distress. His reply to her demonstrated one of disgust when he said;

"You speak as one of the foolish women speaks.
Shall we indeed accept adversity?"

Job 2:10a

Job had an understanding that was lacking in all the other people, which Father God honoured, for we read, *"In all this Job did not sin with his lips."* Job 2:10b

It is accepted that when a person is not in good health, they are more vulnerable to depression and spiral out of control as things progress downward, but Job was not like this. Although he lived what appeared to be a charmed life, he did not take everything he had for granted. He certainly did not appear to be entitled, but accepted the not-so-good times as well as the good times and embraced them equally.

Job could have believed God had betrayed him, but he chose not to. His wife was no encouragement as she would be dealing with her issues, let alone a husband who was suffering all day every day. What God had allowed to take place in this family, for most of us is unthinkable.

The words from Job's wife may have been prompted by Satan. Remember, this is spiritual warfare. For her to say, *"Curse God, and die,"* was not part of the agreement, God had with Satan. If Job had cursed God, he would have lost his righteousness. Keeping the agreement he had with God, was not on Satan's schedule as he would do everything to bring Job down, riding the boundary as close as he dared.

When Satan failed to get to Job through his wife, remember all his sons and daughters were taken, then the next port of call was his friends.

We need to be aware that Satan will use anyone and anything to destroy our relationship with Father God. Those closest to us are usually the first, followed by family and friends. Three friends turn up. Eliphaz the Temanite, Bildad the Shuhite, and Zophar the Naamathite.

Eliphaz the Temanite accused Job of sinning and is being chastened by God, but Job denied this accusation and involvement. Bildad the Shuhite, backed up his friend by telling Job to repent. Job responded with the fact that there was no Mediator as he was the priest, who carried out the sacrifices for others. Zophar the Naamathite agreed with Bildad and said he should repent. After Job responded to each of them, he told them to leave. Job chapters 4 - 14

The friends took offence at Job expecting them to leave. Eliphaz accused Job of foolishness and a lack of good sense. Job was not happy with his pitiless friends. Bildad agreed with Eliphaz and said that the wicked are punished, but Job replied that He trusted God to know best. To add insult to injury, Zophar shared a sermon with Job on the 'Wicked Man'. Job chapters 15-21.

These three badged Job continually until Job silenced them with his defence. Job saw that he was righteous in his own eyes. He justified himself rather than God. Job chapters 22-32:2

While three of his so-called friends were convinced Job had sinned, there was one other, but he was much younger than all of them, so he kept his counsel until they said no more.

"Elihu, the son of Barachel the Buzite, of the family of Ram was aroused against Job; his wrath was aroused, because he justified himself rather than God. Also against his three friends his wrath was aroused, because they had found no answer, and yet had condemned Job." Job 32:2-3

Elihu contradicted Job's friends and then contradicted Job. He proclaimed God's justice, condemned self-righteousness, and proclaimed God's goodness. Elihu was God's servant, in the right place at the right time as God hadn't forgotten His servant Job. Amid all the chaos created by Satan, God watched and monitored everything that took place. Job chapters 32-37.

God used a whirlwind to speak to Job, once the young Elihu had sown the good seed of God (Job 38-40:2). Job answered the words of God with this reply;

> "Behold, I am vile;
> What shall I answer You?
> I lay my hand over my mouth.
> Once I have spoken, but I will not answer;
> Yes, twice, but I will proceed no further."
>
> Job 40:4-5

God challenged Job in verses 40:6 to 41:34. Job was aware of the errors of his ways and repented. He used the following as part of his prayer for forgiveness.

> "I know that You can do everything,
> and that no purpose of Yours
> can be withheld from You.
> You asked, 'Who is this who hides counsel
> without knowledge?'

> *Therefore I have uttered what I did not understand,*
> *things too wonderful for me,*
> *which I did not know."*

Job 42:1a-3

The Lord then instructed Eliphaz the Temanite, Bildad the Shuhite, and Zophar the Naamathite, to bring seven bulls and seven rams and ask Job to offer up a sacrifice and to pray for them. If they were disobedient to God's orders, they could expect the same treatment as Job had experienced. Job 42:7-9

I have briefly explored the Book of Job and found revealed truth that had previously gone unnoticed. The words of Jesus assure us that;

> *"These things I have spoken to you,*
> *that in Me you may have peace.*
> *In the world you will have tribulation;*
> *but be of good cheer,*
> *I have overcome the world."*

John 16:33

We should expect that Satan will do his best to destroy our relationship with Father God. Isaiah gave us a glimpse of the mind of God when he said;

> *"For my thoughts are not your thoughts,*
> *nor are your ways My way."*
>
> Isaiah 55:8

Paul, when writing to the Ephesians reminded them that their daily fight was spiritual, not physical.

> *"For we do not wrestle against flesh and blood,*
> *but against principalities, against powers,*
> *against the rulers of the darkness of this age,*
> *against spiritual hosts of wickedness*
> *in the heavenly places."*
>
> Ephesians 6:12

James, the earthly brother of Jesus, has some words of encouragement when we are experiencing trials and temptations.

> *"My brethren,*
> *count it all joy when you fall into various trials,*
> *knowing that the testing of your faith produces patience.*
> *But let patience have its perfect work,*
> *that you may be perfect and complete, lacking nothing."*
>
> James 1:2-4

Did you notice James wrote, 'when you fall', not 'if you fall'?

Peter in his first epistle wrote to those who had accepted Jesus Christ as their Saviour, that they have a living hope because they are kept by the power of God. Peter continues;

> *"In this you greatly rejoice,*
> *though now for a little while, if need be,*
> *you have been grieved by various trials."*
>
> 1 Peter 1:6

When we pass through a trial, we often feel we are on an island, all alone, that no one else has ever been through the same situation as we are permitted to face. It is ours and ours alone. I am reminded of Paul when writing his first letter to the Corinthians, *"No temptation has overtaken you except such is common to man."* 1 Corinthians 10:13a

When a trial is presented to us, one is required to be selective with who shares their burden. There are those who, with the best of intentions, will give you all the advice they think you need. Maybe they have not been through the waters you are floundering in, but they have the answers. Even though Job had four friends show up, three were of no help at all as they betrayed Job in his time of need.

Their line of reasoning was the acceptable thinking of their day. Sin was the cause of illness. You would remember this line of thinking was still around when Jesus was teaching in the last months of His ministry.

> *"His disciples asked Jesus, saying,*
> *'Rabbi, who sinned, this man or his parents,*
> *that he was born blind?'*
> *Jesus answered,*
> *'Neither this man nor his parents sinned,*
> *but that the works of God should be revealed in him'."*
>
> John 9:2-3

In the beginning, when Job's three friends are urging Job to repent of his sin, although he had not sinned, Job's confession is;

> *Though He slay me,*
> *yet will I trust Him.*
> *Even so,*
> *I will defend my own ways before Him."*
>
> Job 13:15

In the end, when Job's three friends have been rebuked for their thinking, along with Job for his, the Lord dealt with Job concerning his beliefs. His confession had changed too;

> *"I know that You can do anything,*
> *and that no purpose of Yours*
> *can be withheld from You."*

Job 42:2

When we are consumed by any situation we are called to endure, we need to remember the words of the psalmist who wrote;

> *"For His anger is but for a moment,*
> *His favour is for life;*
> *Weeping may endure for a night,*
> *but joy comes in the morning."*

Psalm 30:5

Everything happens for a reason. It may appear hard and the light at the end of the tunnel can't be seen, but trust in God to direct your steps is imperative if you are obediently following the path mapped out for your feet. Don't always listen to well-meaning friends who think they know best, but talk to the Shepherd, not the sheep. You may find as Job did, that some sheep are wolves in sheep's clothing.

The final question to be asked is, "Why did God allow Satan to do this to Job?" These are the questions that the majority will ask, "Why me? Why is this happening to me? What have I done wrong? What did I do wrong?" The fact is that you are probably the innocent party and other situations are happening because God has permitted it. I would share a quote that I read some time ago.

> "Don't worry about the people
> God removed from your life.
> He heard the conversations you didn't,
> saw things you couldn't
> and made moves you wouldn't"

Jesus explained the 'True Vine' to His disciples, and told them how the Father prunes each of His trees to produce the best fruit. (John 15:1-8). This is called the pruning process, where some areas of our lives or even people need to be removed completely, for Father God to perfect His will in us.

When all the bad is stripped away, we may not look very good for some time. Trying to explain to others what we are going through is almost impossible for them to comprehend unless they have been exactly where we are. Remember, if we needed it, God would have let us keep it.

God instigated the conversation with Satan and God used Satan to accomplish a predetermined work in the life of Job. Satan fell into God's trap a second time and was unaware. So, what was God's hidden agenda? Let me share the following verse with you.

> "Elihu, the son of Barachel the Buzite,
> of the family of Ram was aroused against Job;
> his wrath was aroused,
> because Job justified himself rather than God."
>
> Job 32:2

Although Job was protected, rich and prosperous, he had one fault that God chose to correct. Job justified himself rather than being justified by God. When Job was shown the error of his ways, he sincerely sought forgiveness which was obtained and he was right with God.

Your faith, along with your soul, are the two prize possessions that you must protect at all costs. If Satan can do anything to either of these, he will. When situations come your way that you have no explanation for, remember that God has all in control. Remember the following verses when you are struggling.

> "I waited patiently for the Lord
> and He inclined to me,

> *and heard my cry.*
> *He also brought me up out of a horrible pit,*
> *out of the miry clay,*
> *and set my feet upon a rock and established my steps."*
>
> Psalm 40:1-2

> *"Be anxious for nothing,*
> *but in everything by prayer and supplication,*
> *with thanksgiving,*
> *let your requests be made known to God;*
> *and the peace of God,*
> *which surpasses all understanding,*
> *will guard your hearts and minds*
> *through Christ Jesus."*
>
> Philippians 4:6-7

Conclusion.

Spiritual Warfare is a very real and present danger in the life of a person who is committed to Jesus Christ. God permits areas of our life to be refined as we follow His plan and purpose. Decisions made in the spirit world, are of no concern to us, as God has everything in control. Our part is to trust Him through our faith, which we all have a portion given to us. Romans 12:3

God required Job to be refined in his heart attitudes. Although God saw Job as blameless and upright, did not exempt him from refinement.

God in His wisdom, fed Satan with exactly the right thoughts to manipulate him into doing the expressed will of God. Satan was full of pride and did not accept the challenge that he could not have his way with Job. Satan tried his best to persuade God to lift His hand of protection from Job, but God appealed to Satan and his pride issues, and Satan could not resist.

God always has boundaries in place to protect us from the spiritual forces we are not capable of defeating on our own. God knew Job's heart and was confident His will would, in the end, prove a benefit to Job, although Job was unaware.

When Satan came a second time, defeated that he had not accomplished the expectations he had presumed would happen, God then taunted Satan about inciting Him against Job to bring confusion. The boundaries were relaxed a little to protect the life of Job. Satan again took the bait offered by Father God and went his way.

Sickness in most people is a downtime, as many go down the path of despair and depression. For the followers of Jesus, this can be a time of fellowship and reliance on the Holy Spirit to supply the grace so needed to deal with the situation they have found themselves in.

Job appeared to be hard and callous, not grieving as many would. He did not sympathise with his wife but virtually told her to get over it. It would appear that Job was a self-righteous person. His first confession was, *"Thou He slay me, yet will I trust Him. Even so, I will defend my own ways before Him."* Job 13:15

Job appeared to see everything as black and white, not getting emotionally involved. This was a heart attitude that Father God was about to correct. A verse that gave insight into Job's life says, *"In all this, Job did not sin with his lips."* (Job 1:10b). This could infer that the heart of Job was not right in the sight of God.

Job was self-righteous, not God-righteous. Righteousness that comes from a person's own goodness and work is self-righteousness. Job was relying on his own good works to justify himself. This only earns judgement.

Three of Job's friends thought they knew what was causing Job to be sick. They knew something was wrong, but did not have the understanding to find an answer. They thought he had sinned, but there was no proof, so they condemned him.

Elihu had patiently listened to the mature men speak. Considering all he had heard, he was then given not only wisdom but understanding to enlighten Job which enabled Father God to direct His refining power into the heart of Job.

Job accepted the thoughts of God, which changed his confession from one about self-justification to one of reliance and focus on God. Job's reply was, *"I know that you can do anything, and that no purpose of Yours can be withheld from You."* Job 42:2

We all need to accept and not question or reject the refining process God has allowed for our benefit. While we may suffer loss, hardship, pain and much more, if God in His wisdom has chosen to remove someone or something from our life, we should trust Him to know best.

Joseph's Journey.

Joseph was a descendant of Shem, who was one of the blessed sons of Noah. Twelve generations had passed, and Joseph was born into the family of Jacob.

To understand the life of Joseph, we need to discover the history of his family. Joseph's grandfather, Isaac, had twin sons Esau and Jacob, and Jacob was Joseph's father. Esau was the eldest and entitled to the birthright, but Jacob deceived his brother and stole the birthright. Their mother Rebecca also deceived Isaac and encouraged Jacob to visit her brother Laban to find a wife as Jacob would find safety with his uncle's family, and would remove him from Esau's hatred.

When Jacob arrived at the drinking well in the land of Haran, he met Rachel. Love, at first sight, was for both Jacob and the shepherdess. When Jacob met Laban, it was agreed that Jacob would work seven years to marry his daughter Rachel. But when the time came for the marriage, Laban deceived Jacob by substituting the older sister Leah to be his wife. When Jacob realised that he had been deceived, Laban explained that the older daughter married first. To marry Rachel, Jacob would need to work another seven years, but after a week with Leah, he could also take Rachel as his wife.

As the years passed, Leah gave birth to four sons, Reuben, Simeon, Levi, and Judah but, as Rachael had not fallen pregnant, she gave her maidservant Bilhah to Jacob, who gave birth to two sons Dan, and Naphtali. Not to be outdone, Leah, who thought she was past childbearing age, gave her maidservant Zilpah to Jacob who also gave birth to two sons Gad, and Asher. Leah again went into Jacob and gave him another two sons, Issachar, and Zebulun, and a daughter Dinah. One could imagine, after at least eleven years, Rachel, the true love of Jacob was in despair.

> *"Then God remembered Rachel,*
> *and God listened to her and opened her womb.*
> *And she conceived and bore a son.*
> *So she called his name Joseph,*
> *and said,*
> *'The Lord will add to me another son'."*
>
> Genesis 30:22-24

Rachel, after many years, had a son of her own. Because Jacob loved Rachel more than the others, Joseph was his favourite, but unfortunately, this did not go unnoticed.

Joseph's Journey.

Joseph watched as his father Jacob, gathered all his family and possessions, and using camels, fled away from his grandfather, Laban. Twenty years had passed since his father had first met his grandfather. When Joseph's grandfather caught up with his father, he watched as his grandfather angrily searched their tents and possessions for an idol that belonged to him. He noticed the anger subside, as they covenanted with each other about the foreseeable future and watched as his grandfather left and returned to his home.

Even though Joseph was a young child, he was aware of events in his family. On another occasion, his father Jacob appeared to be concerned about meeting his brother, Uncle Esau. He watched as his father prayed to God, confessing his past and then asking for protection. Joseph brought to mind some words his father said;

> *"For You said,*
> *'I will surely treat you well,*
> *and make your descendants*
> *as the sand of the sea,*
> *which cannot be numbered for multitude'."*
>
> Genesis 32:12

Joseph remembered his father, who took his aunt Leah, his mother and all the other children and crossed over the Ford of Jabbok. He noticed his father did not stay with them but was alone on the other side. When Joseph awoke in the morning, he saw his father was limping. As Jacob re-joined them, he recalled how his father hurriedly arranged everyone in order. The two maidservants were in front with their children, then Leah and her children, behind them all, as for complete protection, Joseph stood beside his mother Rachel.

This was the first time he had seen or met Uncle Esau. Although his father Jacob appeared to be afraid, Joseph watched as they both embraced and wept together. While Joseph was too young to understand what the past held for his father and uncle, he understood that reconciliation had taken place between them both. His uncle Esau returned to Seri, where he lived, and they continued their journey to Succoth where they built a house and shelter for the livestock.

Joseph noticed his father was very angry with two of his older brothers, Simeon and Levi and had something to do with Dinah his sister. Not long after, his father Jacob addressed the whole of his family and gave strict orders to be followed.

Joseph's Journey.

> *"Put away the foreign gods*
> *that are among you,*
> *purify yourselves,*
> *and change your garments."*
>
> Genesis 35:2b

The family obeyed Jacob and then packed up everything and travelled to Bethel. While they were living at Bethel, his father told them that God had changed his name from Jacob to Israel. Joseph heard the promise that God had given to his father to accompany his name change. God said;

> *"I am God Almighty.*
> *Be fruitful and multiply;*
> *The land which I gave Abraham and Isaac*
> *I give to you; and your descendants*
> *after you I give this land."*
>
> Genesis 35:11-12

Joseph was content to be with his mother Rachel, who cared for him and his father. Jacob favoured Rachel and Joseph more than the others as he saw the love his father showed for his mother and how she responded to his affection. But the time came, not far from Bethlehem, that his mother Rachel died while giving birth to his brother, whom his father called

Benjamin. His father was distressed as he missed Rachel and so did Joseph, as nobody loved him as she did. He was about eight years old when Rachel died.

Joseph's life changed dramatically. Without a mother, he was cared for by the women in the family and his bond with Benjamin grew strong. When Joseph was seventeen years old, he was with the sons of both the maidservants when feeding the flock. Joseph was not impressed with their behaviour and told his father Jacob, what he had seen and heard but his father understood more than his son.

When Joseph was about seventeen and Benjamin was eight, Jacob presented Joseph with a *'Coat of Many Colours'*. One could imagine that Jacob gave this to Joseph on Benjamin's birthday as a remembrance of his mother's death. Although the maths don't line up exactly, neither of the boys was born on the same day. But we are not told.

Joseph noticed his brothers were envious, and could not even speak to him peaceably. They interpreted the actions of their father, as a complete slight on all of them. What Jacob had done brought so much rebellion from the other ten brothers. This robe or coat was a very special garment that signified a father's love and favour toward Joseph, as well as the destiny he would one day fulfil.

The gift of the coat was seen as a divine favour of God, of receiving the birthright that typically went to the eldest son. It wasn't a work garment like his brothers would wear, but rather an elaborate work of art that was made to stand out. It spoke of nobility, not hard work. Their father had effectively promised the family headship to Joseph.

From experience, Jacob had felt slighted because Isaac favoured Esau over him. If anyone should understand the frustration of favouritism, it should've been him, but instead of breaking the cycle, he ups the ante. No wonder the brothers rebelled.

Joseph was gifted with the interpretation of dreams. God gave Joseph a dream which he shared with his brothers, which only made them more antagonistic toward him and increased their hatred. So, what had Joseph shared?

> *"There we were,*
> *binding sheaves in the field.*
> *Then behold,*
> *my sheaf arose and also stood upright;*
> *and your sheaves stood all around*
> *and bowed down to my sheaf."*
>
> Genesis 37:7

His brothers said to him;

> *"Shall you indeed reign over us?*
> *Or shall you indeed have dominion over us?"*
>
> Genesis 37:8a

The animosity between Joseph and his older brothers increased. But Joseph's dreams and the prophecy from the Lord were not over as he shared another dream with his brothers, and also with Jacob, his father

> *"The sun and the moon,*
> *and the eleven stars bowed down to me."*
>
> Genesis 37:9b

Jacob was not amused with the dreams of Joseph. He may have been his favourite, but replied;

> *"What is this dream that you have dreamed?*
> *Shall your mother and I and your brothers*
> *come and bow down to the earth before you?"*
>
> Genesis 37:10b

While his brothers envied him, his father committed to memory what Joseph had dreamt.

Jacob called Joseph and asked him to locate his brothers who were tending their sheep, and bring back a report. He sent him out of the Valley of Hebron to Shechem. When Joseph was a good distance away, he saw his brothers and the flock of sheep.

When Joseph greeted his brothers, instead of them being pleased to see him, they grabbed him and tore his coat off him.

"What are you doing," said a very frightened Joseph.
"We've had enough of you and your dreams, O favoured one," replied one of the brothers.
"Please give me back my coat," said Joseph.
"You won't be needing your precious coat where you are going," came the reply.

They all manhandled Joseph to a nearby pit and threw him headlong into the darkness. Fortunately for Joseph, the pit was dry.

"Please let me out. I promise I won't tell father," came the mournful cry from Joseph.

But the cries went unheeded by all the brothers. Presently a company of Ishmaelites appeared riding their camels on their way to Egypt. From the pit, Joseph heard Judah say;

Betrayal

> *"What profit is there if we kill our brother*
> *and conceal his blood?*
> *Come, let us sell him to the Ishmaelites,*
> *and let not our hand be upon him,*
> *for he is our brother and our flesh."*
>
> Genesis 37:26-27

The other brothers listened to Judah, so when the Ishmaelites passed by, they drew Joseph up out of the pit and sold him to them for twenty shekels of silver, and the Ishmaelites took him to Egypt.

When Joseph arrived at Egypt he was sold as a slave to an officer of Pharaoh, a captain of the guard by the name of Potiphar. Because the Lord was with Joseph, all that he did prospered which pleased his master. Potiphar recognised the potential in Joseph, so he made him overseer of his house and put everything he had under his authority.

Joseph spent about three years as a slave to Potiphar but during this time, he was harassed by his wife who was attracted to him. She asked him on numerous occasions to lie with her, but Joseph refused. Joseph's rejection offended her so she accused him of sexual misconduct. Potiphar believed his wife's lies, took Joseph and put him in the Pharaoh's prison, a place where the king's prisoners were confined.

The truth was that Joseph had resisted her advancements out of respect for God and her husband.

> *"But the Lord was with Joseph*
> *and showed him mercy,*
> *and He gave him favour*
> *in the sight of the keeper of the prison."*
>
> Genesis 39:21

Favour continued to follow Joseph, wherever he went and with whatever he did. Because the prison-keeper trusted Joseph, he put all things under his authority, even the other prisoners. He didn't think he even needed to check what Joseph was doing, as the Lord was with him and prospered all that he did.

Joseph continued to serve the keeper of the prison and his fellow prisoners with respect and was courteous to all. One day, Joseph noticed two new prisoners had arrived, the head butler and the baker who had offended the king of Egypt. They had made Pharaoh angry, so he had them both imprisoned. The captain of the guard put Joseph in charge of both these men, and Joseph served them, as they were in his custody.

After the first night, Joseph checked and they were both sad, so Joseph asked them to tell him why. They had both had dreams but the meanings evaded them. Joseph said to them;

> *"Do not interpretations belong to God?*
> *Tell them to me, please."*
>
> Genesis 40:8b

The butler shared his dream with Joseph who was able to give him a favourable interpretation. Within three days, he would be restored to his position as butler to Pharaoh. The baker also shared his dream, but unlike the butler, within three days the baker would be hanged. Joseph asked the butler to remember him when he was restored to his position as he was in prison falsely. However, two full years would pass before the butler remembered Joseph's request.

Pharaoh had gone to bed as he usually did, but this night filled him with fear. He had a dream which he could remember in vivid detail. He slept again and had a second dream, again which he could remember all the details. Now in the morning, his spirit was troubled by these two dreams, so Pharaoh called all the magicians and wise men of Egypt and told them the dreams, but none could offer even the slightest interpretation.

It was now the chief butler who spoke to Pharaoh and reminded him of the time he was imprisoned and how a young Hebrew man was able to give him and the baker a correct interpretation of each of their dreams. Pharaoh immediately sent orders for Joseph to be released and to appear before him, but before presenting himself to Pharaoh, Joseph shaved and changed his clothing.

Pharaoh looked at the young Hebrew man who stood before him and said;

"I have had a dream,
and there is no one who can interpret it.
But I have heard it said of you
that you can understand a dream, to interpret it."
So Joseph answered Pharaoh, saying,
"It is not in me;
God will give Pharaoh an answer of peace."

Genesis 41: 15-16

Pharaoh described both his dreams to Joseph and waited for his reply. Joseph respectfully addressed Pharaoh and repeated to him the words God told him to say. Joseph explained that both dreams had the same theme. But because the dreams were repeated, the severity of the drought would be extreme. A well-formulated plan would be necessary to avoid complete disaster. Joseph continued;

> *"Let Pharaoh select a discerning and wise man,*
> *and set him over the land of Egypt."*
>
> Genesis 41:33.

Joseph had humbled himself not only in the sight of Pharaoh but in the eyes of God. Pharaoh recognised Joseph's wisdom and that the *'Spirit of God'* was with him and agreed with Joseph. Pharaoh, along with all the servants in his house, unanimously agreed to appoint Joseph to enact a plan to safeguard them all. Only Pharaoh was greater than Joseph.

So impressed was Pharaoh with Joseph, that he clothed him in fine linen and gave him his ring to wear and a gold chain, and changed his name from Joseph to Zaphnath-Paaneah. He also gave him a wife Asenath, the daughter of Poti-Pherah priest of On. Joseph was thirty years of age when he appeared before Pharaoh. A lot had happened in thirteen years since Jacob gave him his coat of many colours.

As God had preordained, the famine began, slowly at first but then the full force came to pass. About nine years had passed, and if anyone who had doubts about the interpretation of Pharaoh's dreams would have been thankful that the God of Joseph had spared them the hardship. Five years were left to travel.

During the nine years, Joseph's wife, Asenath, bore him two sons, Manasseh and Ephraim. Joseph chose both names for his boys. Manasseh's name meant 'forgetting' and Ephraim's name meant 'fruitful'. From the names he chose, one could imagine he had forgiven and forgotten what his brothers had done to him as he moved positively forward in his attitude and looked to a fruitful future. Joseph also remembered the words given to his father Jacob, by the Lord.

> *"I am God Almighty.*
> *Be fruitful and multiply;*
> *The land which I gave Abraham and Isaac*
> *I give to you; and your descendants*
> *after you I give this land."*
>
> Genesis 35:11-12

As Joseph was personally involved in the distribution of the stored grain, he watched, as people came to him, asked and paid for their grain. Eventually,

> *"Joseph's brothers came*
> *and bowed down before him*
> *with their faces to the earth.*
> *Joseph saw his brothers and recognised them*
> *and spoke roughly to them."*
>
> Genesis 42:6-7

After inquiring about the region they had come from, he remembered the dreams he had in his teen years and accused them of being spies. After interrogating the ten brothers, he had them put into prison for three days. When the three days had passed, Joseph once again spoke to them.

> *"Do this and live, for I fear God:*
> *If you are honest men,*
> *let one of your brothers be confined to your prison house;*
> *but you,*
> *go and carry grain for the famine of your houses.*
> *And bring your youngest brother to me;*
> *so your words will be verified, and you shall not die."*
>
> Genesis 42:18-20

Joseph communicated with his Hebrew brothers through an interpreter, but as they talked together he understood everything they said. It was Reuben, the eldest who showed the greatest regret for their past act concerning the treatment of Joseph, whom they thought was dead. Joseph was so emotionally moved by their response, that he turned away when tears flowed down his face. Joseph turned back to face his brothers and then carried out his words. He had Simeon bound before them and led away.

Retribution can manifest in many ways. Unbeknown to his brothers, Joseph gave a command to fill their sacks with grain, to restore every man's money to his sack, and to give them provisions for their journey.

Some months had passed, and Joseph was distributing grain. He noticed his brothers had returned and recognised Benjamin who accompanied them. Joseph gave orders that the men were to be escorted to his house and a meal prepared for them all. The brothers were not expecting this reception, and they were sorely afraid as they wondered what would happen to them. They shared their concerns with the steward of Joseph's house who reassured them;

> *"Peace be with you, do not be afraid.*
> *Your God and the God of your father*
> *has given you treasure in your sacks;*
> *I had your money."*

Genesis 43:23

Simeon joined his brothers as water was provided to wash their feet, and feed was given to their donkeys. The servants made all things ready for Joseph to return and dine with the brothers. When Joseph returned, his brothers bowed down before him to the earth. They gave him the best fruits of their land which they had carried with them and a personal present of a little balm, a little honey, spices and myrrh, pistachio nuts and almonds.

Joseph spoke to them through an interpreter and asked them about their well-being and inquired if their father was well and if he was alive. And they answered,

> *"Your servant our father is in good health;*
> *he is still alive."*
> *And they bowed their heads down*
> *and prostrated themselves.*

Genesis 43:28

Joseph was about to pass through the most emotional part of his life because He had the heart of his mother whereas his older brothers had the hearts of their mothers and father. Joseph noticed his brother Benjamin, his mother's son. Joseph asked,

> *"Is this your younger brother*
> *of whom you spoke to me?"*
> *And he said,*
> *"God be gracious to you, my son."*

Genesis 43:29

Joseph was so emotionally moved, that he removed himself from their presence and went into a separate chamber where he wept. After he had washed his face, he returned, restraining himself from any other emotional outburst, and gave the command to *'Serve the bread'*. Joseph sat by himself, the Egyptians in their reserved seating, because it was an abomination for them to eat with Hebrews, and the brothers in a separate place.

Deception was a part of Joseph's plan when dealing with his brothers, like the way they treated him so many years previous. Joseph commanded that the sacks be filled and the money once again be placed in the mouth of every sack. He also commanded that his special silver cup be placed in Benjamin's sack. The orders were carried out and the brothers left on their loaded donkeys as soon as the morning dawned.

Joseph watched as his brothers left Egypt for the trip home, but they were unaware of what was about to happen. Joseph gave orders to his steward to overtake his brothers and search their sacks as his silver cup was missing. If the cup was found, then the one who was responsible for the theft would die, while the others would become his slaves.

The steward completed his task. When the cup was found in Benjamin's sack, the brothers tore their clothes, reloaded their donkeys and returned to the city, to Joseph's house. When Joseph asked them the reason for committing the theft, they fell before him on the floor.

> *Then Judah said, "What shall we say to my lord?*
> *What shall we speak?*
> *Or how shall we clear ourselves?*
> *God has found out the iniquity of your servants;*
> *here we are, my lord's slaves,*
> *both we and he also with whom the cup was found."*
>
> Genesis 44:16

But Joseph replied;

> *"Far be it from me that I should do so;*
> *the man in whose hand the cup was found,*
> *he shall be my slave.*
> *And as for you,*
> *go up in peace to your father."*
>
> Genesis 44:17

Hearing what Joseph had said, Judah came close to Joseph and asked him permission to speak. This enabled Judah to intercede for Benjamin and their father. Judah offered his life for Benjamin's, as the loss would kill their father. Judah could not bear to face his father Jacob without the youngest son with them. One could only imagine Joseph's emotions as he watched his brothers fulfil the dreams he had, when in their company so many years before, bow down before him.

Joseph commanded, *"Make everyone go out from me!"* When he was alone, Joseph wept so loud that all the Egyptians and the house of Pharaoh heard him, such was the depth of feelings for those who had betrayed him, whom he had trusted and loved. Joseph, with no interpreter present, spoke to his brothers in Hebrew, their language, as he revealed himself to them as Joseph, the brother they had sold into slavery, but it was God's long-term plan to preserve life.

The brothers were speechless and found it hard to comprehend all that had transpired and the guilt each had carried for so many years, especially the betrayal to their father Jacob about his son Joseph. Joseph then released his brothers to tell Jacob that he was alive and well. As there were still five years of famine to go, Joseph provided carts and stock to transport Jacob and all his family to Egypt, where he would provide everything. This said, they left to face their father Jacob.

Joseph oversaw those purchasing the grain when Judah came to him so, Joseph made ready his chariot and accompanied Judah to the land of Goshen, where he met his father Jacob. When Joseph saw his father, they immediately embraced and wept for a great while. Jacob said to Joseph;

> *"Now let me die,*
> *since I have seen your face,*
> *because you are still alive."*
>
> Genesis 46:30

The family settled in the land of Goshen where they prospered, while some of the brothers were appointed to be chief herdsmen over Pharaoh's flocks. Joseph was eager for Pharaoh to meet his father Jacob so, a suitable time was arranged and Jacob presented himself to Pharaoh and blessed him. Pharaoh's curiosity was aroused and he asked Jacob how old he was. Jacob replied;

> *"The days of the years of my pilgrimage*
> *are one hundred and thirty years;*
> *few and evil have been the days of the years of my life,*
> *and they have not attained to the days of the life*
> *of my fathers in the days of their pilgrimage."*
>
> Genesis 47:9

Joseph was wise in all his dealings before God and with man. Eventually, all the reserve money the people had was used, so they came to Joseph to seek grain. He offered to buy all their livestock in exchange for grain. But after a year had passed, they again came seeking a solution to their plight as all they had left was themselves and their land, which Joseph purchased for Pharaoh. Only the priests were exempt, as the priests were allotted rations, so they did not sell their land. Then Joseph said to the people;

"Indeed I have bought you and your land this day for Pharaoh.
Look, here is the seed for you,
and you shall sow the land.
And it shall come to pass in the harvest
that you shall give one-fifth to Pharaoh.
Four-fifths shall be your own,
as seed for the field and for your food,
for those of your households and as food for your little ones."

Genesis 47:23-24

With all that had transpired, Jacob clung to the promise God had given him many years previous. When he sensed his time of life was nearing its end, he called Joseph and made him vow that when the time came, he would ensure that his body would be taken and buried with his fathers in the cave that is in the field of Machpelah, which is before Mamre in the land of Canaan. Joseph agreed to do as he had been asked and swore to Jacob his wishes would be carried out.

As the ageing process took a firm hold on Jacob, Joseph took both his sons, Manasseh and Ephraim to Jacob. Jacob outlined the covenant God had given him to Joseph.

> *"Behold, I will make you fruitful and multiply you,*
> *and I will make you a multitude of people,*
> *and give this land to your descendants*
> *after you as an everlasting possession."*
>
> Genesis 48:4

Jacob asked who the two young men Joseph had with him were so, Joseph introduced his two sons, Manasseh and Ephraim to their grandfather, Jacob. Then Jacob said to Joseph,

> *"I had not thought to see your face;*
> *but in fact,*
> *God has also shown me your offspring!"*
>
> Genesis 48:11

Jacob then blessed both of Joseph's sons but gave the blessing of the firstborn to the second. This displeased Joseph, but Jacob explained,

"I know, my son, I know.
He also shall become a people,
and he also shall be great;
but truly his younger brother shall be greater than he,
and his descendants shall become a multitude of nations."

Genesis 48:19

Then Jacob said to Joseph,

"Behold, I am dying,
but God will be with you
and bring you back to the land of your fathers.
Moreover I have given to you one portion above your brothers,
which I took from the hand of the Amorite
with my sword and my bow."

Genesis 48:21

Jacob summoned all his sons to his bedside where he addressed them. As Jacob spoke to each, nothing was held back as he laid the bare facts before each one. He told them their faults and where they had displeased him but also encouraged them for things they had done. Each one was in turn told how their future days would unfold. When he looked at Joseph, his favourite, he shared with loving kindness about his future.

Betrayal

"Joseph is the fruitful bough, a fruitful bough by a well;
His branches run over the wall.
By the God of your father who will help you,
and by the Almighty who will bless you
with blessings of heaven above.
The blessings of my ancestors,
up to the utmost bound of the everlasting hills.
They be on the head of Joseph,
and on the crown of the head of him
who was separate from his brothers."

Genesis 49: 22, 25, 26

When Jacob had completed blessing each one, he drew his feet up into the bed, breathed his last, and was gathered to his people. After Jacob's death, Joseph spoke with Pharaoh who permitted him to bury Jacob in the cave in the field of Machpelah, which is before Mamre in the land of Canaan. Many accompanied Joseph and shared his loss as Jacob was laid to rest with his ancestors in the cave. After the time of mourning was completed, Joseph and those who accompanied him, returned to Egypt.

As the actions of their past travelled with the brothers, guilt and fear took over. Revenge was in their thinking that now Jacob was dead, maybe Joseph would pay them back for what they had maliciously said and done toward him.

Joseph's Journey.

So concerned were the brothers, that they sent a messenger to Joseph asking for forgiveness for their past transgressions. When Joseph received their message, he wept. When the brothers came and met him face to face, they bowed before him and said, *"We are your servants."* But Joseph replied,

> *"Do not be afraid, for am I in the place of God?*
> *But as for you, you meant evil against me;*
> *but God meant it for good,*
> *in order to bring it about as it is this day,*
> *to save many people alive.*
> *Now therefore, do not be afraid;*
> *I will provide for you and your little ones."*
>
> Genesis 50:19-21a

Joseph lived to the age of one hundred and ten years and Joseph saw Ephraim's children to the third generation and Manasseh's children were also brought up on Joseph's knee. Joseph knew when his time was to leave this life. He said to his brethren,

> *"I am dying; but God will surely visit you,*
> *and bring you out of this land*
> *to the land of which He swore to*
> *Abraham, to Isaac, and to Jacob."*
>
> Genesis 50:24

Joseph took an oath from the children of Israel, that they would not leave him in Egypt when they were called by God to leave and go to the land He had promised to his ancestors.

> *"So Joseph died, and they embalmed him,
> and he was put in a coffin in Egypt."*
>
> Genesis 50:26

Conclusion.

From the earliest accounts of Joseph's life, it could appear that as the favoured child, his behaviour towards his brothers was often inappropriate. He shared his dreams with his family which irritated them and produced animosity toward him. Because Joseph related what some of his half-brothers were doing when minding the sheep to Jacob, his relationship with them all decreased even further.

Confronted with death by his brothers, must have proved a great wakeup call to Joseph. His attitude changed when he became a slave and was denied all the luxuries he had previously enjoyed. Joseph never forgot the teaching of his mother Rachel, about care and attention for others, also respect for those over him, and their property.

Joseph's actions may have been misunderstood, as his emotional state in his later life's situations, became obvious. Was he more concerned than what his actions as a child portrayed? Did the loss of Rachel at the age of eight have consequences for him that were never addressed? Was this the reason he chose to irritate those of his family? We are not told.

What we are told is that God repeatedly elevated Joseph as a leader by helping him earn the trust of high government officials and the people.

- Potiphar. Genesis 39:4
- The Prison Warden. Genesis 39:22-23
- The Butler. Genesis 41:9
- Pharaoh. Genesis 41:39-44
- He also earned the trust of the people. Genesis 47:25

In his leadership, Joseph consistently honoured God by his character in the following ways. His values, behaviour, self-discipline, consistency, a heart of compassion, and a passionate purpose.

Joseph would understand the meaning of the present given to him by his brothers (Genesis 43:11). Balm was a special healing oil from Gilead. The wild honey, spices and myrrh were highly prized in Egypt for cosmetics, perfume, incense, and embalming the dead. Pistachio nuts were a rare delicacy, and almonds grew wild in Canaan. All the gifts proved they had returned to Canaan.

Betrayal

Hygiene was of the utmost importance to the Egyptians, more so than the children of Israel. As true Egyptians did not eat with Hebrews, the fact that Joseph invited his brothers into his home, and gave them water to wash their feet along with food for their donkeys, reassured the brothers they were guests, not prisoners. As guests, they are provided the customary hospitality of water for washing and food for their animals.

Although there is no tribe of Joseph, his inheritance was split and given to his two sons, Ephraim and Manasseh. The other ten tribes are, Ruben, Simeon, Judah, Dan, Naphtali, Gad, Asher, Issachar, Zebulun, and Benjamin. The tribe of Levi had no land allotted to them because they had a special calling to hold the priesthood and perform ordinances under the law of Moses. Because of this calling, they lived among all the other tribes and were not counted in the same way. Israel was generally considered to have twelve tribes plus the Levites.

Joseph was one of Jacob's sons, his favourite. His brother's jealousy enveloped him and had disastrous outcomes for his future. When they sold him into slavery, Joseph grew up quickly. He made better choices and relied on God to supply him with wisdom and understanding. Joseph allowed his light to shine continually, no matter his circumstances.

Joseph's Journey.

Joseph's life is a testimony to the sovereignty and grace of God for those who live faithfully and righteously. Joseph remained faithful and trusted God to deliver him from all tribulations. Joseph showed great faith, faithfulness, long-suffering, patience and temperance. While he had several serious setbacks and appeared to be placed in impossible situations, he always found a way to keep his covenant promises as he trusted God.

A foreshadow of Jesus can be found in the life of Joseph when he is approached by Judah who intercedes for the life of his younger brother, Benjamin. Judah offers his life in exchange for the life of Benjamin. In the future, Jesus would be born of the tribe of Judah. Just as Judah offered his life in exchange for Benjamin, Jesus would offer His life in exchange for the sin of mankind.

Gideon. Mighty Man of Valour

The story of Gideon began when an Angel of the Lord came and sat under the terebinth tree which was in Ophrah, which belonged to Joash the Abiezrite, while his son Gideon threshed wheat in the winepress, to hide it from the Midianites. Wheat was normally threshed on the roof in plain sight, where the wind would blow away the husks, but because of the oppression, Gideon hid in the cellar, as he felt secure hidden down in the enclosed winepress.

Ancestry.

Gideon was the son of Joash, from the Abiezrite clan in the tribe of Manasseh. Joseph, his ancestor, had two sons, Manasseh and Ephraim by his wife Asenath. The tribe of Manasseh descended from one of Joseph's two sons. Joseph chose both names for his boys. Manasseh's name meant 'forgetting' and Ephraim's name meant 'fruitful'. Their grandfather, Israel blessed both sons but gave the blessing due to Manasseh, the firstborn, to the second son Ephraim. Because Joseph was displeased, Israel explained;

"I know, my son, I know.
He also shall become a people,
and he also shall be great;
but truly his younger brother shall be greater than he,
and his descendants shall become a multitude of nations."

Genesis 48:19

The Oppressors

The tribe of Manasseh was smaller in size than that of his younger brother Ephraim. The children of Israel had left the path directed by God and continued on their way in disobedience to the covenant previously agreed to by their ancestors. As a way of correction, Father God had delivered them, into the hands of the Midianites for seven years. The question to be asked is, "Who are the Midianites?"

Abraham was married to Sarah who gave her Egyptian handmaid to her husband to provide the promised son. This was not God's plan, and Haggar bore a son whom they called Ishmael. Sarah did have a son some twenty years later and they called him Isaac. After the death of Sarah, Abraham, who is about 135 years old, married Keturah (Genesis 25:1), who according to Jewish tradition was a descendant of Noah's son Japheth.

Keturah gave Abraham a further six sons. Their names were Zimran, Jokshan, Medan, Midian, Ishbak, and Shuah. The Midianites were the descendants of Midian. All six brothers followed their father's belief in the ways of Father God until Abraham died. 1 Chronicles 1:32-33

The Midianites, along with the Amalekites, who were descendants of Amalek, a grandson of Esau, the older brother of Jacob, attacked the chosen children of Israel, and plundered their fields and livestock, leaving nothing for Israel. All the fighting and killing was one great family feud, whose ancestry roots go back to Noah's three sons, Shem, Japheth and Ham, those blessed and cursed.

The Conquest

As the scene has been set, the Angel of the Lord appeared to Gideon and said;

> *"The Lord is with you,*
> *you mighty man of valour."*

Judges 6:12

Gideon may have been timid and shy, as he hid away in the cellar, but he was not backward in coming forward when he spoke to the Angel of the Lord. He had questions for the Angel and expected answers. When dealing with God's messengers, we are never ready for the predetermined will of the Father. When Gideon asked how he could defeat the Midianites, the Angel replied;

Betrayal

> *"Go in this might of yours,*
> *and you shall save Israel*
> *from the hand of the Midianites.*
> *Have I not sent you?"*
>
> Judges 6:14

Gideon shrank back as he did not see himself as a warrior but God did. His clan was the weakest in Manasseh, and as he was the youngest in his family, his self-esteem was at an all-time low. The Angel continued to encourage him, and assured Gideon, that because He would be with him, the Midianites would be defeated by him as one man.

Although Gideon did not understand all the Angel had told him, his self-confidence had gathered momentum. He required further encouragement so asked the Angel to stay until he had prepared and presented an offering to God. The Angel agreed and Gideon left, prepared the offering and presented it to the Angel under the terebinth tree. The angel of God said to him;

> *"Take the meat and the unleavened bread*
> *and lay them on this rock, and pour out the broth.*
> *Then the Angel of the Lord*
> *put the end of the staff that was in His hand,*

and touched the meat and the unleavened bread;
and fire rose from the rock and consumed the meat
and the unleavened bread.
And the Angel of the Lord departed out of his sight."

Judges 6:20-21

The Lord continued to reassure Gideon he was called for a purpose. On the same night, the Lord gave instructions to Gideon, to tear down his father's altar to Baal, and the wooden image of Asherah, who represented the Canaanite goddess. He was to build an altar to God and use the wood of the image, to offer a sacrifice. Gideon was obedient to the revealed will of God, but he waited until the night-time because he feared his father's household and the men of the city.

In the morning, when the men of the city saw what had happened to their idol god, they asked who was responsible. When told it was Gideon, they told Joash, Gideon's father, to bring him out so they could kill him. Joash stood his ground and said;

"Would you plead for Baal?
Would you save him?
Let the one who would plead for Baal
be put to death by morning!

> *If Baal is a god, let him plead for himself,*
> *because his altar has been torn down!"*
>
> Judges 6:31

Only a short time had passed and the Midianites and the Amalekites crossed over and encamped in the Valley of Jezreel. When their encampment was made known to Gideon, *"the Spirit of the Lord came upon Gideon."* In Hebrew these words mean, *'The Spirit of the Lord clothed Himself with Gideon'*. The Spirit empowered this divinely appointed leader and acted through him to accomplish the Lord's saving act on behalf of His people.

Gideon took and blew the trumpet. When the trumpet sound was heard, it signalled a battle was about to happen. The sound was calling God's people to unite and was also a reminder to God of His covenant promise to defeat the enemy and save them. The men of Abiezrites, his clan, gathered behind him. Gideon also sent messengers to Asher, Zebulun, and Naphtali, neighbouring tribes of the children of Israel to join them in their battle.

It would have been daunting for Gideon, as he came out of hiding in a cellar to the leader of thousands. One victory over an altar and statue, at night, was not enough to convince Gideon, even when the Holy Spirit possessed him. There is still the gift we were all given by God, and that is the freedom to choose.

Gideon needed constant encouragement that the will of God would succeed so, Gideon simply petitioned God for assurance that He would save Israel. Gideon placed a fleece on the threshing floor and simply asked that the dew be on the fleece only and the surrounding ground be dry. As the request was granted, Gideon came a second time and requested that the fleece would be dry and the ground wet and this was also granted. Gideon had his confirmation.

These petitions were not to test God. Gideon did not request the sign of the fleece to determine God's will but to gain deepened assurance. Through divine revelation, Gideon already knew he was appointed to deliver Israel. He required confirmation of the Lord's presence and power to enable him to accomplish the task.

When all the fighting men were assembled, Gideon led them out and camped on the north side of the invaders, by the hill of Moreh in the valley. Moreh was a prominent hill located at the entrance of the Valley of Jezreel. The Lord said to Gideon;

Betrayal

> *"The people who are with you are too many*
> *for Me to give the Midianites into their hands,*
> *lest Israel claim glory for itself against Me,*
> *saying, 'My own hand has saved me'."*

Judges 7:2

At the Lord's word, Gideon encouraged men to return home, and twenty-two thousand left leaving ten thousand to fight the battle. But the Lord required Gideon to further reduce the number so they all gathered at the water in the valley and everyone was told to drink. Some knelt and drank, while others lapped from their hands. Those who lapped from their hands were three hundred men. God chose these three hundred to fight His battle so, Gideon sent the others home. The difference between the two groups was that some stayed alert at all times, whereas the others relaxed.

One could imagine that when thirty thousand fighting men were gathered together, expectations would be high regarding victory. As the numbers reduced to three hundred, even those who were left would have cause to be concerned as to what their leader was doing. The company of three hundred were well aware that their enemy;

> *"Would come up with their livestock and their tents,*
> *coming in as numerous as locusts;*

both they and their camels were without number;
and they would enter the land to destroy it."

Judges 6:5

The Lord was aware of Gideon and his need for continued encouragement so, He told him to take his servant Purah and go to the enemy's camp and listen to what they said. Gideon did as he was instructed and came to the outpost where the armed men were. As they came near, Gideon heard a man telling another man about a dream he had. He said;

"I have had a dream: To my surprise,
a loaf of barley bread tumbled into the camp of Midian;
it came to a tent and struck it so that it fell and overturned,
and the tent collapsed."

And the other man answered;

"This is nothing else but the sword of Gideon
the son of Joash, a man of Israel!
Into his hand God has delivered Midian
and the whole camp."

Judges 7:13b-14

Gideon worshipped the Lord as his faith had been reinforced amid what could be confusion and fear.

But what was the meaning of the dream? Barley was considered an inferior grain, which was used by the poor and the loaf symbolized Israel, who appeared inferior and smaller in number than the Midianite army. The tent represented the entire Midianite camp.

Gideon was filled with enthusiasm when he heard the interpretation so when they returned to their camp, he rallied the three hundred men into three groups. All they had was a trumpet, and an empty pitcher, which contained a torch. Gideon told them all to follow his lead. When the time to attack would come they were to shout;

> "The sword of the Lord, and of Gideon."
>
> Judges 7:18b

Gideon and his men were ready just before the middle watch and waited as all the people in the camp were sleeping or sleepy. Suddenly and without warning, Gideon and all his men simultaneously smashed the pitcher, placed the trumpet in their right hand and the torch in the other, then cried out, *"The sword of the Lord and of Gideon."* While Gideon's army stood their ground, they watched as mass confusion and hysteria spread throughout the camp of Midianites, as each turned his sword on the other. Then the whole army ran and cried out and fled.

When the outcome of the battle was known throughout Israel, men from Naphtali, Asher, and all Manasseh, pursued the Midianites, killing many and seized the water places. While most praised Gideon for his heroic efforts and faith in Father God, the men of Ephraim reprimanded him sharply for not involving them from the beginning. To understand this attack on Gideon, we would need to take a few steps back into a past encounter.

Joseph, the son of Jacob, met his father in his old age in Egypt. Joseph had his two sons with him, Manasseh and Ephraim. They were to share the land given to Joseph but under their names. When Jacob blessed Joseph's sons, he gave the blessing reserved for the first son, Manasseh to Ephraim. This displeased Joseph, but Jacob explained to Joseph when he said the following;

"I know, my son, I know.
He also shall become a people,
and he also shall be great;
but truly his younger brother shall be greater than he,
and his descendants shall become a multitude of nations."

Genesis 48:19

Over the years that passed, the tribe of Ephraim had grown stronger and greater than that of Manasseh. Gideon replied to them saying;

> *"What have I done now in comparison with you?*
> *Is not the gleaning of the grapes of Ephraim*
> *better than the vintage of Abiezer?"*

Judges 8:2

Gideon compared the two tribes and realised what was most important. God had clearly shown that numbers were not necessary to obtain a victory, but faith and trust in the One who had ordained or called his servant to obedience. When Gideon said, *"The gleaning of the grapes,"* he was probably referring to Ephraim's mop-up work following the initial battle. Was this a pride issue for the leaders of Ephraim? We are not told. The *"Vintage of Abiezer,"* was referring to Gideon's involvement in the victory over the Midianites. As he was the least, he saw that they in every way outshone him.

But Gideon was not finished with this brother's tribe. He continued;

> *"God has delivered into your hands*
> *the princes of Midian, Oreb and Zeeb.*
> *And what was I able to do in comparison with you?"*
> *Then their anger toward him subsided when he said that."*

Judges 8:3

Gideon and his three hundred men continued to pursue the Midianites who fled, but there was resistance from his fellow countrymen who would not support Gideon and his men in their quest. When Gideon returned after they had captured Zebah and Zalmunna, the two Midian kings, he dealt severely with the men of Succoth, as he taught them a lesson, with thorns of the wilderness and briers. When he came to Penuel, he tore down their tower and killed the men of the city. Gideon talked with the two kings, and because they had killed his brothers, took a sword and killed them both.

Gideon's Ephod

After the conquest was over, the men of Israel wanted Gideon to rule over them. But Gideon declined the offer. He knew that his wisdom and understanding came from the indwelling presence of Father God or as we would say, 'The indwelling of the Holy Spirit'. The writer to the Hebrews listed Gideon as one of the heroes of faith. Hebrews 11:32

Gideon requested that the people surrender to him all the golden earrings from the plunder as they belonged to the Ishmaelites. The question to be addressed is, "How do the Midianites, descended from Abraham and Keturah, become Ishmaelites, who descended from Ishmael, the slave son of Haggar?" While there is no direct answer, the following verse of scripture may give a clue as to a possible answer.

> *"But Abraham gave gifts to the sons*
> *of the concubines which Abraham had;*

and while he was still living he sent them eastward,
away from Isaac his son,
to the country of the east."

Genesis 25:6

One could reason that Abraham wanted no religious interference to encroach on God's promised seed, Isaac. To protect Isaac, most of his household was sent away just before Abraham died. But this did not include Ishmael, as he stayed with Isaac and buried their father Abraham with Sarah in the cave at Machpelah. While Isaac went to live in Beer Lahai Roi, Ishmael lived in the area from Havilah as far as Shur, which is east of Egypt as you go toward Assyria. Genesis 25:18a

As the areas border with each other, as nomadic groups, they could move and settle, taking their religious views with them. As Gideon took the crescent ornaments from around the camels' necks, they represented the moon god, worshipped by many pagan people during this time. One would then accept that the Midianites had not followed the path of the patriarch Abraham, but like most, turned away and worshipped other gods.

Gideon's request was granted and the gold was gathered which was made into an ephod and set it up in the city of Ophrah. The Ephod was to be worn when God's people were led in the worship of Yahweh, and in thanksgiving for all He had done for them. Gideon wanted the ephod to be a testimonial to all Israel that God is God, and God alone is to rule over them, and they are to worship Him. But as with most objects, the focus changed, and we read;

> *"All Israel played the harlot with it there.*
> *It became a snare to Gideon*
> *and to his house."*
>
> Judges 8:27b

Idolatry entrapped people and lured them away from the worship of the true God. Not only does Israel begin to worship Gideon's ephod as an idol, but it also ensnared Gideon and his family. There was peace in Israel for 40 years during Gideon's life, but as soon as he died of old age, the Israelites again turned to worship the false god Baal-Berith and ignored the family of Gideon. Judges 8:33

> *"Thus the children of Israel*
> *did not remember the Lord their God,*
> *who had delivered them*
> *from the hands of all their enemies on every side;*
> *nor did they show kindness to the house of Jerubbaal (Gideon)*
> *in accordance with the good he had done for Israel."*
>
> Judges 8:34-35

Conclusion

Gideon was the son of Joash, from the Abiezrite clan in the tribe of Manasseh and lived in Ephra (Ophrah). As a leader of the Israelites, he won a decisive victory over a Midianite army despite a vast numerical disadvantage, leading a troop of three hundred men.

We learn from the life of Gideon that every experience in life is a test and every trial in the lives of God's people is tailored to draw us closer to Him. When we experience tough times, instead of looking at them as if God was punishing us, try to see them as God's gift of grace.

The story of Gideon in the Bible demonstrated how God can shape any of us into strong leaders if we are willing to take one step, even if small, of faith at a time.

God uses the weak things of this life to confound the mighty. It is obvious from the start that in Gideon, God chose a weak, fearful man. Gideon is characterized by fear and inadequacy and has little or no self-confidence. God came to him as he was beating wheat in a wine press, hiding, because he was afraid.

The children of Israel felt insignificant, just like Gideon who was in despair, bent over in a pit to conceal his meagre produce. Yet God called Gideon *'a mighty warrior'* to show both Gideon and the people of Israel they would soon be rescued by God's hand. The people made to feel small, would soon stand tall and mighty again!

Gideon was also a leader with insight. He had the wisdom to see the issues, and understanding to know what lay ahead. God gave him knowledge into the weak hearts of the Midianites. Gideon led with confidence, and the three hundred selected men were willing to follow him because of this.

We need to remember that Gideon was the youngest of his family. It would appear that the kings of Midian, Zebah and Zalmunna, killed all of Gideon's brothers, because *'they looked like him and resembled the son of a king'*. When Gideon heard their reasoning, he killed them both. Judges 8:18-19

When God calls you, He has a purpose and will give you the power to accomplish the task. God does not look at people as men see them, for God can use anyone in His service. Gideon will always be remembered as a great leader and a man of valour because God knew that through his obedience, His purpose would be served. God doesn't call us for any of our perceived skills.

Several lessons can be gleaned from the story of Gideon.
- The mission hasn't changed.
- God sometimes does big things in unlikely ways.
- It's not your battle but the Lord's.
- God will accomplish His plan.
- God wants leaders to walk in confidence by faith, not by sight.

Gideon's faith in God grew with each assignment. He wholeheartedly trusted God and grew into a mighty man who brought peace to his people. Gideon had tested God and God had shown Gideon His power. As Gideon's trust and willingness to follow God grew, God tested Gideon's faith when He reduced the Israelite army from thirty-two thousand to three hundred men.

So, what can we say about the life of Gideon? His life stands to show us that God sees the best in us when we don't. Gideon was successful in his call because he allowed God to use him. We can do the same. Gideon's story reminds us that the tough times can be the times when we experience the most growth.

Samson. Man of Power and Weakness

Samson's story of betrayal began when 'A man of God' with the countenance of an 'Angel of God', appeared to his barren mother, and told her that she would become pregnant and have a son. While his mother's name is unknown, Samson's father's name was Manoah, whose father was Dan, one of the twelve sons of Jacob.

The Angel of the Lord appeared to Manoah's wife twice and once to Manoah. After a conversation between the three, Manoah accepted without question what the Angel said and inquired about the boy's rule of life and his work. Both parents were required to carry out in obedience, to what was revealed as the will of God for their child, even before he was conceived. They were told,

> "Please be careful not to drink wine or similar drink, and not to eat anything unclean.

For you shall conceive and bear a son.
And no razor shall come upon his head,
for the child shall be a Nazarite to God from the womb;
and he shall begin to deliver Israel
out of the hand of the Philistines."

Judges 13:4-5

"So the woman bore a son
and called his name Sampson;
and the child grew, and the Lord blessed him.
And the Spirit of the Lord began to move upon him
at Mananeh Dan between Zora and Eshtaol."

Judges 13:24-25

    While Samson was blessed from the womb, this did not prevent him from making wrong decisions. He had the choice to follow God's ways or to do what was right in his own eyes. As an only child, he probably did whatever he wanted without retribution. When he saw a Philistine woman who pleased him, he requested his parents to *"Get her for me as a wife"* (Judges 14:2b). His parents would have known and taught him that he was to choose a bride from his people, but when this was suggested, he retaliated by saying,

> *"Get her for me,*
> *for she pleases me well."*
>
> Judges 14:3b

Samson was telling his parents, "She is right in my sight." Had he forgotten the fifth commandment?

> *"Honour your father and your mother,*
> *that your days may be long upon the land*
> *which the Lord your God is giving you."*
>
> Exodus 20:12

Both parents respected their son and did what he had asked because we are told,

> *"But his father and mother did not know*
> *that it was of the Lord that He was seeking*
> *an occasion to move against the Philistines."*
>
> Judges 14:4

Samson found himself alone in the vineyards of Timnah, where a young lion attacked him. The Spirit of the Lord came mightily upon him and he tore the lion apart although he had no weapon, but he didn't tell his parents. Sometime later when he returned to Timnah, he noticed in the carcass of the lion he had killed, was a swarm of bees and honey. He took some and ate it and gave some to his parents to eat, but he chose not to tell them where he obtained the honey.

During the seven-day feast that accompanied his wedding, Samson posed a riddle to thirty of the young men. If they could answer the riddle correctly in seven days, he would give them thirty linen garments and thirty changes of clothing. But if they could not explain the riddle, then they would give him thirty linen garments and thirty changes of clothing. They all agreed and Samson said,

> *"Out of the eater came something to eat,*
> *and out of the strong came something sweet."*
>
> Judges 14:14

The young men had no idea of the answer, so they went to his bride and threatened to burn her and her father's house if she did not give them the solution. Because she was afraid for her family, she cried continuously for the seven days of the wedding feast until on the last day, Samson told her the answer to his riddle. Just before sunset, the young men told Samson the answer, but he replied,

> *"If you had not plowed with my heifer,*
> *You would not have solved my riddle."*
>
> Judges 14:18b

Samson knew his wife had betrayed him to her people, so he went and killed thirty of a neighbouring town's men and gave their clothes to those who had threatened his bride's household. Samson was extremely angry and returned to his father's house. Because he did this, the father-in-law gave his bride to his companion, who had been his best man.

When Samson finally returned to be with his wife, the ugly truth of what the father-in-law had done, surfaced. His anger was rekindled and burned within him. In retaliation, Samson captured three hundred foxes, tied their tails together, set a lighted torch in the middle of their tails and sent them into the fields which burnt the standing grain, as well as the vineyards and the olive trees.

The Philistines were outraged and wanted to know why the fields had been set alight. When they were told Samson burnt the fields because his father-in-law had given his wife to another, they burned the woman and her father as a sacrifice to their god Dagon, who was their god of fertility and grain. As the Philistines had completed this atrocity, Samson killed many of them, then went and dwelt in the cleft of the rock of Etam.

Three thousand men of Judah arrived to arrest Samson for fear of Philistine retaliation. He surrendered to them on the condition they would not kill him. They bound and led him away to the camp of the Philistines. When the Philistines saw him bound, they came out shouting against him, but the Spirit of the Lord came mightily upon Samson. He took a fresh jawbone of a donkey and killed a thousand men with it.

Samson trusted the Lord to supply his needs. Because he was thirsty, he cried out to the Lord and said,

> *"You have given this great deliverance*
> *by the hand of Your servant;*
> *and now shall I die of thirst and fall*
> *into the hand of the uncircumcised?"*

Judges 15:18

God heard his grumbling and split the rock, which provided water for him to drink, then his spirit returned, and he revived. Samson made his way to Gaza where he saw a harlot and went to her. Although a plot to kill Samson failed, his exploits were far from over.

Samson continued on his journey and came to the Valley of Sorek where he fell in love with a woman by the name of Delilah. Each of the lords of the Philistines offered her eleven hundred pieces of silver to betray Samson's secret to his great strength. Delilah tried three times to find out about Samson's strength, and three times he failed to tell her the truth. When she persisted a fourth time, he told her all his heart, so she lulled him to sleep on her lap and engaged a Philistine to cut off his seven locks of hair.

When the locks of hair had been removed, she then taunted him and his strength left. She said, *"The Philistines are upon you, Samson!"* So, he awoke from his sleep, and said,

> *"I will go out as before, at other times,*
> *and shake myself free!"*
> *But he did not know that*
> *the Lord had departed from him.*

Judges 16:20

> *"Then the Philistines took him and put out his eyes,*
> *and bought him down to Gaza.*
> *They bound him in bronze fetters,*
> *and he became a grinder in the prison.*
> *However, the hair of his head*
> *began to grow again after it had been shaven."*

Judges 16:21-22

The lords of the Philistines paid Delilah for betraying Samson and decided to have a great celebration and sacrifice to the god Dagon, who was their god of grain and fertility. When their hearts were merry, what better entertainment could they have than toying with the one they captured. Samson was led into their temple and after he had performed for them, they placed him between the two pillars that supported the temple for all to see.

Samson asked the boy who led him by the hand, *"Let me feel the pillars which support the temple so that I can lean on them."* The boy did as he asked, and then Samson called to the Lord, saying;

"O Lord God,

remember me, I pray!

Strengthen me, I pray,

just this once,

O God, that I may with one blow

take vengeance on the Philistines for my two eyes!

Let me die with the Philistines!"

Judges 16:28, 30a

Samson took hold of the two pillars that supported the temple, and braced himself against them, one on his right and the other on his left, and he pushed with all his might, and the temple fell on the lords and all the people who were in it. With this action, Sampson killed both himself and more Philistines than he had killed during his life.

> *"And his brothers and all his father's household*
> *came down and took him,*
> *and brought him up and buried him in the tomb*
> *of his father Manoah.*
> *He had judged Israel twenty years."*
>
> Judges 16:31

God's Plan and Purpose for Samson.

There is a saying, "Three strikes and you're out!" While this is a baseball term, it has been applied to many of life's situations. The life of Samson was no different except that he had a calling and purpose from his mother's womb to the day he would die. This was a life commitment for Samson, not just a specific time or season. When the name Samson is mentioned, five things are associated with his life. They are;

- Nazarite Vow.
- Strength.
- Hair.
- Eyes.
- Obedience.

While his parents took their promise from the Angel of the Lord seriously, and followed the instructions meticulously, when Samson was of age, certain conditions of his **'Nazarite Vow'** were dismissed, as his desires took pride of place. We need to understand what the Nazarite commitment meant for the person who had chosen this way of life. We read the following which explains what was expected of the Nazarite.

A man or woman consecrates an offering to take the vow of a Nazarite, to separate themselves to the Lord,
- *They shall separate themselves from wine and similar drink.*
- *During their separation, they shall not eat from the grapevine.*
- *No razor shall come upon their head.*
- *They shall not go near a dead body.*
- *They'll not make themselves unclean or their family members.*
- *All the days of their separation shall be holy to the Lord.*

Numbers 6:2-8

What Samson took for his life's motto was, "I will do what is right in my eyes" (Judges 14:3b). He did not consult the Lord to understand what was right in His eyes. Not until his last breath, did he acknowledge God by understanding that he was weak and dependent on God's strength.

While Samson knew he was strong, he was unaware of the amount of **strength** the Lord would at times, enable him to use. He did not understand that the *'Spirit of the Lord'* was the source of his unusual ability. When he tore apart the young lion that was attacking him, he was alone in the vineyards of Timnah. Why was he even there? This was a forbidden area for him. Satan doesn't change his tactics, as you would remember, Eve was at the *'Tree of the Knowledge of Good and Evil'* when she sinned. Samson did not share this incident with his parents.

His marriage feast to the Philistine woman lasted seven days, but just before sundown, the answer to his riddle was given to him. The *'Spirit of the Lord'* came mightily upon Samson, and he went down to Ashkelon, where he used his strength to kill thirty of the men and gave their clothes to the thirty guests assembled for the feast.

The *'Spirit of the Lord'* was not always present when Samson acted. The last recorded event was when Samson took a fresh jaw bone from a donkey and killed a thousand men in retaliation for burning his Philistine wife and her father.

But there was one other time when Samson, in repentance, asked God to renew his strength. His prayer was answered as he pushed with all his might, and the pillars holding up the roof of the temple of Dagon fell and killed all who had gathered for the celebration, including the lords of the Philistines who had paid Delilah to betray Samson. I wondered if Delilah was the guest of honour, as it was she who had betrayed Samson. But we are not told.

Samson's **hair** was platted into seven locks (Jud. 16:19b). What is significant about the hair of the head? In ancient Hebrew culture, hair was considered a symbol of strength, beauty and spiritual devotion or consecration to God. Hair held significant cultural and symbolic value and was often regarded as a symbol of power, masculinity, and sometimes shame, especially among rulers and leaders. Samson possessed immense physical strength as long as he did not cut his hair, but His long hair became a representation of his power, and he lost his strength when it was cut off.

Baldness or hair loss was seen as a sign of weakness or divine punishment. One biblical example illustrating this is the story of the prophet Elisha, when a group of disrespectful youths mocked him for being bald, he called upon bears to attack them, signifying the serious consequences attributed to making fun of someone's lack of hair (2 Kings 2:23-24). On the other hand, hair could also be a source of shame. During war or captivity, shaving or shearing hair was a common way to humiliate and dehumanize individuals. Samson's hair was cut off, stripping him of his power and led to his capture.

Why Samson had seven locks of hair is unclear. To have locks was not uncommon as the Philistines paid no attention to him having his hair styled in this fashion. It was only his confession to Delilah to prove his love for her, that enabled her to betray him to the lords of the Philistines. While he loved her, she lusted for money.

From the first recorded event in Samson's life, his *eyes* had been his downfall. The root cause of Samson's fall was his weakness to the temptation of the flesh and eventually, his lust for women would be his undoing. The disciple John in his first epistle wrote the following which would sum up the life of Samson.

> *"Do not love the world or the things in the world.*
> *If anyone loves the world,*
> *the love of the Father is not in him.*
> *For all that is in the world,*
> *the lust of the flesh,*
> *the lust of the eyes,*
> *and the pride of life,*
> *is not of the Father but is of the world."*
>
> 1 John 2:15-16

Unbeknown to Samson, he submitted to all three temptations, the lust of the eyes, the lust of the flesh, and the pride of life. John refers to the *'lust of the flesh'*, as the desire to satisfy any of the physical needs. The *'lust of the eyes'* were the women who pleased his eyes, whom he desired to own or possess. The essence of the *'pride of life'* is anything that exalts oneself above God, wherein we boast in arrogance and worldly wisdom. The Philistines removed his eyes, which were the root cause of his failing in his God-ordained calling.

Many of Samson's ancestors chose not to include **obedience** in their covenant with God. The majority did their own thing and disobeyed God's commandments. Samson should have been taught by oral tradition, about his ancestor Cain and the situation that confronted him when his altar failed to please God. What the Lord spoke to Cain contained wisdom that could be used in any situation.

> *"If you do well,*
> *will you not be accepted?*
> *And if you do not do well,*
> *sin lies at the door.*
> *And its desire is for you,*
> *but you should rule over it."*

Genesis 4:7

Samson had spiritual blindness, as he saw everything was right in his eyes. Judges 14:3b

Another part of the Nazarite vow was the abstinence from wine. This was not just the consumption of fermented grapes but more was expected as the vow says;

"He shall separate himself from wine and similar drink;
he shall drink neither vinegar made from wine
nor vinegar made from similar drink;
neither shall he drink any grape juice,
nor eat fresh grapes or raisins.
All the days of his separation he shall eat nothing
that is produced by the grapevine, from seed to skin."

Numbers 6:3-4

The question to be asked is why was Samson in the vineyards of Timnah? For him, this should have been a no-go area. The Lord sent a messenger in the form of a young lion to make Samson aware of what he was doing. The lesson was two-fold as the slaying of the lion demonstrated his strength, but later would also produce a valuable lesson for him to learn from, and to once more remind him of his Nazarite vows.

When Samson returned to the vineyards, he noticed the carcass of the slain lion and saw a swarm of bees using the carcass as a hive to produce honey. He took and ate some of the honey and also gave some to his parents but did not tell them where he had obtained the honey. This may appear innocent, but the understanding of what Samson had done, the implications for others and the lesson Samson failed to learn, show that he chose to be spiritually blind.

The first thing to note was that Samson should not have been in the vineyard, whether he ate the grapes or not. The second was the fact that he touched a dead carcass which was forbidden, let alone take honey from the bees within it. The third thing to note was he gave some to his parents, which not only broke another vow but he deceived them both by not telling them where he obtained the honey.

It should have been obvious to Samson, that the carcass represented the Philistines whom God would destroy through His strength. The honey represented his bride who was sweet to him and he lusted for her. In other words, the Lord showed Samson the error of his way and he chose to completely ignore the spiritual significance revealed in the situation and God's warning. He was in total violation of his calling.

A piece of advice for those who would know the revealed will of God is, 'The way up is down'. Samson, because of his superior attitude and disregard for his covenant, would need to go down to the depths of despair to find true repentance. This would be a painful, humiliating and frustrating path, but Samson was called to walk the way God directed for him. While Samson chose his way, God directed his steps.

Humility has a price tag and does not come cheap for some. Samson's eyes were removed and he ground grain constantly in the prison to which he was confined, wearing fetters of bronze. One could only imagine the ridicule, torment, and abuse he would have suffered from his oppressors. The greatest humiliation was probably being taken to the temple of Dagon as entertainment in front of thousands of Philistines. The great Samson had changed as we read,

> *"Then Samson said to the lad who held him by the hand,*
> *'Let me feel the pillars which support the temple,*
> *so that I can lean on them'."*
>
> Judges 16:26

Samson was led by a lad who held him by the hand. This man of power had finally bowed to the Lord with a complete humbleness of heart. He found himself in the company of vicious men and women who would only do him harm out of revenge for what he had done to them. He was in the end, led as a lamb to the slaughter. Isaiah would later pen the words;

> *"The wolf also shall dwell with the lamb,*
> *the leopard shall lie down with the young goat,*
> *the calf and the young lion and the fatling together;*
> *and a little child shall lead them."*
>
> Isaiah 11:6

Samson's Life Foreshadows Events in the New Testament.

Samson was to begin the defeat of the Philistines. John the Baptist paved the way for Jesus.

Samson, John the Baptist and Jesus' births were all foretold by angels.

Samson and John the Baptist were born to barren women, and Jesus was born to a virgin.

Samson defeated a lion. Jesus defeated Satan, who is described as a 'roaring lion'.

Samson sacrificed himself and killed thousands. Jesus sacrificed Himself to give life for the called.

The Church and the Seven Locks of Hair.

In Western civilisation, the church seems to be a type of Samson. Jesus, through the Holy Spirit, established the church which would someday be His bride, but over time, Satan has sifted the church to be wanting in so many areas. The church should be empowered by the Spirit when engaged with the world, but Jesus revealed to the Apostle John exactly what the end-time church would be like when he wrote to the angel of the church at Laodicea or the Lukewarm Church.

"I know your works, that you are neither cold nor hot.
I could wish you were cold or hot.
So then, because you are lukewarm,
and neither cold nor hot,
I will vomit you out of My mouth.
Because you say, 'I am rich, have become wealthy,
and have need of nothing' and do not know
that you are wretched, miserable, poor, blind, and naked.
I counsel you to buy from Me gold refined in the fire,
that you may be rich; and white garments,
that you may be clothed,
that the shame of your nakedness may not be revealed;
and anoint your eyes with eye salve,
that you may see."

Revelation 3:16-18

Jesus instructed the church to buy eye salve to anoint their eyes so that they could see because they were blind to the things of God. Their spiritual eyes were blind. The City of Laodicea was noted for producing a salve for the curing of eye disorders. Their church desperately needed the grace that regenerates Spirit-illumined eyes of the heart. Paul when writing his second letter to the Corinthians encouraged them to *walk by faith and not by sight.* 2 Corinthians 5:7

Have you noticed that this is all about sight and blindness? Samson's problems began with his eyes, eventually, they were removed and he became physically blind. Jesus knew what lay in wait for future generations, who would be similar to those of the past who grumbled and disobeyed continually, except for those who are the called. He said,

> *"Come to Me,*
> *all you who labour and are heavy laden,*
> *and I will give you rest.*
> *Take My yoke upon you and learn from Me,*
> *for I am gentle and lowly in heart,*
> *and you will find rest for your souls.*
> *For My yoke is easy and My burden is light."*
>
> Matthew 11:28-30

The Seven Locks of Hair and Christianity.

Let me share with you the seven basics of Christianity.

- God. A Triune God who consists of three equal parts.
- Jesus Christ. Death and Resurrection.
- The Holy Spirit. God's presence on earth.
- The Bible. God's instructions to us.
- Prayer. Our communication with Father God.
- Grace. The unmerited favour of God on our lives.
- Community. Attach yourself to like-minded people.

The seven pillars of the Church are found in Ephesians 4:4-6.
- One Body.
- One Spirit.
- One Hope.
- One Lord.
- One Faith.
- One Baptism.
- One God and Father.

The seven signs of the Holy Spirit?
- Wisdom.
- Understanding.
- Wise Advice.
- Courage.
- Knowledge.
- Reverence.
- Fear of the Lord.

The seven principles of Faith are found in Colossians 2:6-7.
- Decisiveness.
- Diligence.
- Determination.
- Dedication.
- Discipline.
- Dependence.
- Discernment.

A life of Wisdom is founded on the 'Fear of the Lord'.
- Purity.
- Peacefulness.
- Gentleness.
- Reasonableness.
- Helpfulness.
- Humility.
- Sincerity.

As I pondered all the preceding seven's, a verse of scripture came into my thoughts.

> *"For by grace you have been saved through faith,*
> *and that not of yourselves;*
> *it is the gift of God, not of works,*
> *lest anyone should boast."*
>
> Ephesians 2:8-9

While the Church should have all the characteristics listed, in reality, we are told what to expect people will be like in the last days.

> *"For men will be lovers of themselves, lovers of money, boasters, proud, blasphemers, disobedient to parents, unthankful, unholy, unloving, unforgiving, slanderers,*

> *without self-control, brutal, despisers of good,*
> *traitors, headstrong, haughty,*
> *lovers of pleasure rather than lovers of God,*
> *having a form of godliness but denying its power.*
> *And from such people turn away!"*
>
> 2 Timothy 3:2-5

In our Western Culture, it would appear that our expression of faith is more about us than it is about God. Many have a *form of Godliness but are denying His power*. I guess this is where Jesus describes the final judgement of the Church as a Shepherd separating the righteous sheep from the unrighteous goats. The way the Shepherd distinguishes between the two groups is by examining the sacrificial love they have shown toward the *'least of these, My brothers'*. Matthew 25:40-45

As we have read through the *'Seven Locks of Hair and Christianity'*, the question to be asked is, 'How many locks of hair have been cut off in your church or denomination? In some churches, they have all gone. The Holy Spirit has left and everything goes on just as it always has. Others are struggling and don't know why. Many need to buy eye salve, require an awakening and a renewal of the Holy Spirit or they too will become completely spiritually blind.

What is the real spiritual condition of your church? Are they aware of the Holy Spirit's presence during prayer time or when fellowshipping together? Remember Jesus said,

> *"For where two or three are gathered together*
> *in My name,*
> *I am there in the midst of them."*

Matthew 18:20

How many gather each week or during the week in the expressed Name of Jesus in your church? If this does not occur, why are we surprised that the church has become sounding brass or a clanging cymbal? 1 Corinthians 13b

Jesus gave words of promise and encouragement to the remnant of the Laodicean Church when He said,

> *"Behold, I stand at the door and knock.*
> *If anyone hears My voice and opens the door,*
> *I will come in to him and dine with him,*
> *and he with Me.*
> *To him who overcomes*
> *I will grant to sit with Me on My throne,*
> *as I also overcame and sat down*
> *with My Father on His throne."*

Revelation 3:20-21

What does the story of Samson teach us?

Samson's story is a powerful example of how trusting in God's given strength and abilities can lead to success and victory, but also how pride and arrogance can lead to destruction. We should always remain humble and not allow our pride to hinder the work God has ordained for us to complete.

How God had intended to use Samson as a true Nazarite will never be known as he chose to go his way and do his own thing because it was right in Samson's eyes. The Lord was able to use what Samson had given to Him and turned them into solutions He could use. We need to be careful that we always consult God and wait for the right answer when faced with decision-making, and not do what appears right in our eyes.

Samson shared with Delila the innermost secrets of his heart and she used his genuineness for her benefit. We should also be careful when sharing our God-given thoughts or personal enlightenment with the wrong people who will use them against us. We are told;

> *"Do not give what is holy to the dogs;*
> *nor cast your pearls before swine,*
> *lest they trample them under their feet,*
> *and turn and tear you to pieces."*

Matthew 7:6

We should always obey God's commands and rely on His strength, not our limited resources.

Even though Samson was deceived by Delilah, God forgave Samson and still gave him the strength to fulfil his purpose. We should always remember that we were sought out by God for a reason, as *we did not choose Him but He chose us.* John 15:6

When Samson finally prayed to Father God, he acknowledged his wretched self as he humbled himself before Almighty God in front of the thousands of heathen Dagon worshipers. At the last, Samson prayed his prayer of repentance and God heard his prayer as He does ours and answered Samson's prayer to fulfil His purpose. Samson is remembered for his faith which God renewed just before he died.

There is never a time when we cannot cry out to Father God in a time of desperation, need or joyfulness. God has promised *never to leave us nor forsake us* (Hebrews 13:5b). He also said;

> *"Call to Me,*
> *and I will answer you,*
> *and show you great and mighty things,*
> *which you do not know."*
>
> Jeremiah 33:3

The Nazarite Blessing.

The Lord bless you and keep you;
The Lord make His face shine upon you,
and be gracious to you;
The Lord life up His countenance upon you,
and give you peace."

Numbers 6:24-26

Prayers in the Old Testament.

When people prayed in the Old Testament, I often wonder who they are talking to. The term, *'the Lord'* is frequently used in the Old Testament concerning that part of God who was responding.

I start with the question, "What do we know about God?"

God or the Trinity is made up of three persons. The Father, the Son and the Holy Spirit. Undivided in essence and co-equal in power and glory. In other words, the three make one person but are three separate all at the same time.

Let me share a true-life story with you. I collected my grandson for school and it was obvious something was on his mind. As we travelled along the highway toward his home, he looked at me and said, "Poppy, can I ask you a question?" You never know what an eight-year-old will ask. I replied, "Yes you can. I may not know the answer, but yes. What did you want to ask?" Out of the blue came the response, "Poppy, can you explain the Trinity to me?"

Now, it was obvious to me, as he attended a Christian school, that someone had mentioned the Trinity but had not conveyed the understanding to this eight-year-old. I said, "Just give me a minute please." I said a quick prayer to the Lord, then did my best to explain the Trinity to him. I used the ice, water and steam, but saw no response. I then used a three-legged stool. In desperation, I used the banana, three third pieces altogether in an outer casing. None of these had answered his question.

I needed an explanation that would bring understanding to this young mind. I asked the Lord for guidance and was not disappointed. A few days passed, and I found myself at dinner with my daughter and her family. When the meal was well in progress, I addressed myself to my grandson.

"The other day when I was driving you home from school, you asked me to explain the Trinity to you. I didn't do a very good job, but I have another answer for you."

All eyes were fastened on me and what I was about to say.

"You remember when Nanny was alive, she was my wife."

"Yes," came the reply.

"Your mummy is my daughter, and I am her father."

"Yes."

"You are my grandson. I am three different people but the same person all at the same time."

"Now that makes sense. Thanks, Poppy," came the reply. Everyone began eating again.

This satisfied the inquiring mind of an eight-year-old, the real essence of the Trinity is much more complex.

A second question I asked is, "What else from the Bible do we know about God?"

One could say that God is the original transformer as He can be anything He desires when he chooses. This will become clearer as we progress with the study. Moses, when in the presence of God was told;

> *"You cannot see My face;*
> *for no man shall see Me,*
> *and live."*

Exodus 33:20

The God of the Old Testament was One to be feared. Most people understood that God demanded obedience to His laws, and those who disobeyed wore the consequences. Atonement could only be obtained by the prescribed offering of animals. With the death and resurrection of Jesus Christ,

God's anger was put aside and *'Grace'* was ushered in because of the perfect life and sacrifice of His Son.

A third question would be, "What do we know about Jesus?" Paul when writing to the Philippians wrote the following about Jesus.

> *"Let this mind be in you which was also in Christ Jesus,*
> *who, being in the form of God,*
> *did not consider it robbery to be equal with God,*
> *but made Himself of no reputation,*
> *taking the form of a bondservant,*
> *and coming in the likeness of men.*
> *And being found in appearance as a man,*
> *He humbled Himself and became obedient to the point of death,*
> *even the death of the cross."*
>
> Philippians 2:5-8

On another occasion Jesus said;

> *"I and the My Father are one."*
>
> John 10:30

Jesus was obedient to the will of Father God by separating Himself from them to become the perfect sacrifice, once and for all for mankind. The verse says that Jesus found Himself in the appearance of a man which enables me to say I have no idea what God looks like in the heavenlies. Jesus was transformed into an earthly being as we were formed to be.

When Jesus Christ returns, every eye shall see Him (Revelation 1:7),

> *"For the Lord Himself will descend from heaven with a shout,*
> *with the voice of an archangel,*
> *and with the trumpet of God."*
>
> 1 Thessalonians 4:16a

A fourth question would ask, "What did Jesus say about the Holy Spirit?" John recorded the words of Jesus for our understanding regarding the Holy Spirit. He wrote;

> *"When He, the Spirit of truth, has come,*
> *He will guide you into all truth;*
> *for He will not speak on His own authority,*
> *but whatever He hears He will speak;*
> *and He will tell you things to come."*
>
> John 16:10

John joins all three together when he recalls some other words spoken by Jesus.

> *"But the Helper, the Holy Spirit,*
> *whom the Father will send in My name,*
> *He will teach you all things,*
> *and bring to your remembrance*
> *all things that I said to you."*

John 14:26

The last words Jesus spoke to His disciples at the Ascension, were about the Holy Spirit.

> *"But you shall receive power*
> *when the Holy Spirit has come upon you."*

Acts 1:8a

When teaching and sharing with His disciples, Jesus tried His best to convey to them what was about to happen in the foreseeable future. Jesus knew what He was teaching or sharing would only be understood and realised, once He had been raised from the dead, ascended into heaven and was sitting on the right-hand side of His Father. To Jesus, the following words He uttered gave no hope to those who were listening, but only to those who asked for an explanation. Jesus said;

> *"Seeing they will not see and hearing,*
> *they will not hear nor understand."*
>
> Matthew 13:14

One could only imagine how many of our modern-day preachers, sharers of the 'Word of God', would be disheartened to have this verse as their plan of action or job description. Jesus knew what His role was, and His words would not inhibit the work to be carried out by the Holy Spirit.

While some understanding has been established about Father God, His Son Jesus, and the Holy Spirit, a little more exploration will help establish the work, and purpose of the three.

Let me share the following selected verses from the Old Testament book of Genesis.

"In the beginning God created the heavens and the earth."

Genesis 1:1

"The Spirit of God was hovering over the face of the waters."

Genesis 1:2b

> *"Then God said, 'Let there be light';*
> *and there was light."*

Genesis 1:3

I would share the following selected verses from the New Testament book of the Gospel of John.

> *"In the beginning was the Word,*
> *and the Word was with God,*
> *and the Word was God.*
> *He was in the beginning with God.*
> *All things were made through Him,*
> *and without Him nothing was made.*
> *In Him was the life,*
> *and the life was the light of men."*

John 1:1-4

From both these passages of scripture, we can separate the *'One'* into the *'Three Persons'*. There is *'God'*. *'Jesus'* or the *'Word'*, is also *'Life'*. The *'Spirit of God'* which is the *'Holy Spirit'* is the *'Light of Men'*. It should be noted that while John refers to Jesus as the *'Light'* that came into the world, it was not until Pentecost, that Jesus the *'Light'* was illuminated by the power of the Holy Spirit. For example, if Jesus was the light bulb in the socket, it wasn't until the power was switched on, or became available, that the Holy Spirit brought illumination to the light bulb to reveal all things to believers.

When Jesus came to earth as the light of men, He had the light of men within Himself to be released. Only after Pentecost, the light of men within Jesus became illuminated.

Creation.

All three, God, Jesus and the Holy Spirit, were involved in creation. God created the heavens and the earth (Genesis 1:1), but He had two helpers. The Spirit of God hovered over the face of the waters (v2a), and Jesus spoke as He is the *'Word'* (v3).

God had ordained what was to be created for time and eternity. As the Holy Spirit passed over the chaotic substance we call the world, the observation was realised for mankind and his eternal existence. It was then that Jesus as the *'Word'*, spoke the words of the Father, and creation took place. Each had a part to play in making our habitable world once more exist.

Adam formed.

All three were involved when Adam was formed. After God had finished creating everything, with the help of the other two, He rested. God then chose to form a man. Jesus enacts the Father's plan, took a spirit and clothed it in the dust of the ground, then formed a man. The Holy Spirit also played His part in representing Father God. He who has the power, *"Breathed into his nostrils the breath of life; and man became a living being."* Genesis 2:7

All three were required to work together to form what God had predestined to be His chosen people, *"Kings and priests, to give God glory and dominion forever and ever."* Revelation 1:6

The Lord God.

In Genesis 2:8 to chapter 3:24, the *'Lord God'* is introduced to scripture as God had previously declared that no one can see God's face and live, we can conclude that the *'Word'*, or work part of the three is meant here, along with the One to provide life or power.

When we read the account of the planting of the garden of Eden (Genesis 2:8-25), followed by the fall of man (Genesis 3:1-24), the words *'Lord God'* are used. The Garden wasn't created, as the creative acts of God had finished. The garden was planted. As the working part of God is Jesus, one could imagine He took on a working form when planting the garden. It was in this environment that Adam was placed to tend and care for it (v15).

The *'Lord God'* spoke directly to Adam with instructions as to what he was allowed to do. This was obedience to the known will of God. The *'Lord God'* also formed Eve for Adam (v21). It was also the *'Lord God'* who called to Adam, asking where he was. Adam and Eve also *"Heard the sound of the Lord God walking in the garden in the cool of the day."* Genesis 3:8.

This would be Jesus who is monitoring everything and talks to Adam and Eve, and eventually, the serpent, because Jesus is the *'Word'*. A Spirit would not make noise when walking in a garden. Both Adam and Eve heard the *'Lord God'* walking in the garden.

We can now say that while God is in control, Jesus does the work, and the Holy Spirit provides the power to achieve God's desired results.

The Angels.

At other times, angels were assigned God-given tasks when dealing with people although, some acted because of their selfish interests and intents. The angels we are told about in the Bible are Gabriel, Michael, Lucifer, Abaddon (Apollyon), and the Angel of the Lord. There are many angels not mentioned by name, who were sent by God for a specific purpose. There were also the seven angels John wrote to in the Book of *"The Revelation of Jesus Christ"*.

Gabriel appeared to Daniel (Daniel 8:16), having the appearance of a man interpreted the Vision Daniel had received. Gabriel appeared a second time and gave understanding to Daniel about the Vision (9:21). It was Gabriel who appeared to Zacharias in the temple, and told him about his barren wife conceiving a child (Luke 1:19). Mary was next when Gabriel proclaimed to her, she had been chosen to give birth to the long-awaited Messiah. Luke 1:26

Michael is one of the seven archangels and the guardian champion of Israel. He is first mentioned when aiding Gabriel in a battle against the king of Persia (Daniel 10:13). Michael always supported Gabriel in his conquests (v21). Michael is involved in end-time prophesy, during the tribulation period before the return of Jesus Christ (Daniel 12:1). The following verse records the dispute Michael had with the devil over the body of Moses.

> *"Michael the archangel,*
> *in contending with the devil,*
> *when he disputed about the body of Moses,*
> *dared not bring against him a reviling accusation,*
> *but said, 'The Lord rebuke you!'."*

Jude 9

Michael was acquainted with the role of a protector, as well as standing for what was right.

> *"And war broke out in heaven:*
> *Michael and his angels fought with the dragon;*
> *and the dragon and his angels fought,*
> *but they did not prevail,*
> *nor was a place found for them in heaven any longer."*
>
> Revelation 12:7

Lucifer, who was full of lust, was a fallen angel because he wanted to sit on God's throne and be like the Most High (Isaiah 14:12-15). He is also associated with satan and the devil.

Abaddon or Apollyon are the same angel. Abaddon, a Hebrew name meaning 'Destruction', and Apollon, a Greek name meaning 'Destroyer'. He was the king in the bottomless pit or Abyss. A fallen angel from heaven is the unidentified demonic being, possibly satan, who was given the key to the bottomless pit and released the demonic beings. Revelation 9:1-11

The *'Angel of the Lord'*, would appear to be the most active of all the angels. He is referred to in both the Old and New Testaments. Refer to the *'Angel of the Lord Appearances'* chart. In the Old Testament, he appeared to Abraham, Daniel, David, Eliezer, Elijah, Esther, Ezekiel, Hannah, King Hezekiah, Isaac, Jacob, Jehoshaphat, Jeremiah, Job, Jonah,

Joshua, Manoah, Moses, Noah, Rebekah, Solomon, and Zachariah. In the New Testament, he appeared to Zacharias, Joseph, the shepherds, who rolled away the stone, Philip, Peter and Herod.

The Angel of the Lord spoke to Moses in the burning bush and was present when guiding the children of Israel out of Egypt in the form of a pillar of cloud and fire. He also was seen several times by Zachariah in various forms in the visions he received. Horses, Measuring Line, High Priest, Lamp Stand, Olive Trees, Flying Scrolls, and the Four Chariots. The deliverance of Israel followed.

When exploring the scriptures about the appearances of the *'Angel of the Lord'*, two other statements he made stood out. The first was with Abraham and Isaac.

> *"Then the Angel of the Lord*
> *called to Abraham a second time out of heaven,*
> *and said: 'By Myself I have sworn, says the Lord,*
> *because you have done this thing,*
> *and have not withheld your son,*
> *your only son'."*
>
> Genesis 22:15-16

"*By Myself I have sworn,*" can only refer to God, Jesus or the Holy Spirit. No other created being could make this statement. As Jesus is the *'Word'*, He is reassuring Abraham that what has been agreed in heaven will happen. 1 John 5:7-8

The second statement is to make the announcement to Manoah's wife that she, although barren, would conceive and bear a son. Manoah's response was;

> *"O my Lord, please let the Man of God*
> *whom You sent come to us again*
> *and teach us what we shall do*
> *for the child who will be born."*
>
> Judges 13:8

So many positive responses to what the *'Angel of the Lord'* had told his wife. His prayer was answered, and the Man appeared to his wife a second time, not Manoah, and she ran and told him. Manoah followed his wife to where the Man was. Did you notice that the husband and wife were talking to a Man?

> *"When he came to the Man, he said to Him,*
> *'Are You the Man who spoke to this woman?'*
> *And He said, 'I Am'."*
>
> Judges 13:11b

"I Am." Previously, Moses inquired from the *'Angel of the Lord'*, who had appeared to him in the burning bush (Exodus 3:1-6), by whose authority should he tell the children of Israel decreed the future plans for them? The response came;

> *"And God said to Moses,*
> *'I AM WHO I AM'.*
> *And He said,*
> *'Thus you shall say to the children of Israel,*
> *'I AM has sent me to you'."*
>
> Exodus 3:14

Jesus was the only other One named in the Bible who used the title *'I AM'*. This then poses the question, "Is Jesus the *Angel of the Lord?*" While we are told that Jesus, after the Ascension sat down at the right hand of God (Mark 16:19) until His enemies were made His footstool (Hebrews 10:13), there is absolutely no reason why Jesus could not continue to be active in the lives of people, along with the Holy Spirit, just as Michael was a backup to Gabriel.

Over the years, the 'angel of death' is well known for the part he played on the night before the Exodus of the children of Israel leaving Egypt and Pharoh's control or slavery. When you read the story, it would appear that Jesus passed through Egypt and brought death to those who were not protected by the blood on the doorposts. Exodus 12:1-12

This appeared to conflict with the purpose of Jesus when He said, *"I have come that you may have life and have it more abundantly"* (John 10:10). When we realise that Jesus was talking to the called, those who chose to love and serve Him, then the unsaved will suffer consequences they would have chosen to accept because they chose not to accept Jesus Christ as their Lord and Saviour.

The suggestion has been made that the *'Angel of the Lord'* could be any heavenly being who was charged with doing the direct will of God. Even Satan, a fallen angel, was used by God to perform certain things.

- David. 1 Chronicles 21:1,
- Job. 1:12; 2:6,
- Saul. 1 Samuel 16:14.

But we are not told.

Mankind.

As with the forming of Adam, we are a trinity. We have a body, spirit and soul and are made in the likeness of God.

> *"Then the Lord God said,*
> *'Behold, the man has become like one of Us,*
> *to know good and evil'."*
>
> Genesis 3:22a

We were formed for the glory of God and to be obedient to Him in all ways. Paul when writing his first letter to the Corinthians said;

"Don't you know that your body is the temple of God?"
1 Corinthians 6:19

When we speak and work, Jesus operates through and guides us. When we are prompted to speak words over people or pray for others, that is the Holy Spirit. When people look at us, what or whom do they see? We want them to see Jesus reflected in us. When we exhibit the fruit of the Spirit, such as love, kindness, and gentleness, (See Galatians 5:22-25), that has nothing to do with us, but what the Holy Spirit has achieved through our obedience to Father God, through Jesus and the Holy Spirit.

Our body is the temple of Father God so, what we speak out of our mouth, should be the words of Jesus, as we know;

"For out of the abundance of the heart the mouth speaks."
Matthew 12:34b

Our mind or thoughts are prompts given to us by the Holy Spirit and also the evil powers. We have been given free will to choose what we cast out and what we keep as our thoughts feed our heart. The twofold nature of man is always at war with each other. The things we want to do, we don't do, and the things we don't want to do, we do. Romans 7:13-23.

Our soul is the most prized possession given to us. We should protect the soul until our last breath. This is the dwelling place of Father God or should be. Jesus shared the following words with His disciples as to what they should expect when persecution would overtake them. Jesus said;

> *"Do not fear those who kill the body*
> *but cannot kill the soul.*
> *But rather fear Him*
> *who is able to destroy both*
> *soul and body in hell."*

Matthew 10:28

Isaiah recorded some thoughts of Father God to help us in our everyday lives and dealing with others so that He would receive the praise and glory.

> *"Is this not the fast that I have chosen:*
> *To loose the bonds of wickedness,*
> *To undo the heavy burdens,*
> *To let the oppressed go free,*
> *And that you break every yoke?*

Betrayal

Is it not to share your bread with the hungry,
And that you bring to your house the poor who are cast out;
When you see the naked, that you cover him,
And not hide yourself from your own flesh?

Then your light shall break forth like the morning,
Your healing shall spring forth speedily,
And your righteousness shall go before you;
The glory of the Lord shall be your rear guard.
Then you shall call, and the Lord will answer;
You shall cry, and He will say, 'Here I am.'

If you take away the yoke from your midst,
The pointing of the finger, and speaking wickedness,
If you extend your soul to the hungry
And satisfy the afflicted soul,
Then your light shall dawn in the darkness,
And your darkness shall be as the noonday.

The Lord will guide you continually,
And satisfy your soul in drought,
And strengthen your bones;
You shall be like a watered garden,
And like a spring of water, whose waters do not fail.

Those from among you
Shall build the old waste places;

You shall raise up the foundations of many generations;
And you shall be called the Repairer of the Breach,
The Restorer of Streets to Dwell In.

If you turn away your foot from the Sabbath,
From doing your pleasure on My holy day,
And call the Sabbath a delight,
The holy day of the Lord honourable,
And shall honour Him, not doing your own ways,
Nor finding your own pleasure,
Nor speaking your own words."

Isaiah 58:6-13

What we are required to do should reflect Jesus as we should let the Holy Spirit guide our words, not using or speaking our own.

The Holy Spirit.

Jesus said, *"Whatever you ask in My name, I will do."* That is because the Holy Spirit has prompted you to ask and because the three in heaven agree as one, it is granted by the Father. They can't oppose themselves as this is confusion, and confusion only comes from the evil one. John when writing his first epistle says;

"For there are three that bear witness in heaven:
the Father, the Word, and the Holy Spirit;

and these three are one.
And there are three that bear witness on earth:
the Spirit, the water, and the blood;
and these three agree as one."

1 John 5:7-8

Paul when writing to the Romans, assured them that Jesus was making intercession for them. Nothing has changed. Jesus is making intercession for us.

"It is Jesus Christ who died,
and furthermore is also risen,
who is even at the right hand of God,
who also makes intercession for us."

Romans 8:34

Our responsibility is to be sure what we speak or have spoken is Holy Spirit prompted, not our own words, wants or desires.

People Who Prayed in the Old Testament.

Many of the psalms of praise sung to Father God, thanking Him for delivering the people from trouble, are classed as prayers. In this section, I have chosen to deal with only those who prayed or petitioned Father God silently.

The Old Testament records twenty-one people whose prayers are provided for our contemplation. They are Abraham (Genesis 18:16-33), Daniel (9:1-19), David (17 Psalms), Eliezer (Genesis 24:12-14), Elijah (1 Kings 18:36-40), Esther (4:10-17), Ezekiel (37:3a), Hannah (1 Samuel 1:10), Isaac (Genesis 25:21), Jacob (Genesis 32:9-12), Jehoshaphat (2 Chronicles 20:6-12), Job (13:20-14:22, 40:4-5, 42:2-6), Jonah (2:2-9), Joshua (10:12), Jeremiah (20:7-18), King Hezekiah (2 Kings 19:15-19), Moses (Psalm 90), Noah (Genesis 9:25-27), Rebekah (Genesis 25:22), Samson (Judges 16:28, 30), and Solomon (1 Kings 3:6-9).

These people had an intermate relationship with the God they knew, as each one expressed a heartfelt plea for those in their care. Let us take each one briefly and examine their prayer. As Job has already been dealt with previously, only a summary will be mentioned. Last is David who will be looked at in much more detail covering the spiritual experience of his life under the heading, 'David's Life of Prayer'.

Abraham. Genesis 18:16-33

Abraham interceded on behalf of the evil city of Sodom, as he bargained with God for the safety of those who were living there. God was willing to grant Abraham's petition for the sake of ten righteous people, but God knew the hearts of the residents, and even ten out of possible thousands were not righteous.

Daniel. 9:1-19

Daniel maintained a vibrant prayer life, praying three times a day from his early days (Daniel 6:10). After a decree had been signed by King Darius, that whoever petitions any god or man for thirty days, except the king, shall be thrown into the den of lions, Daniel continued to carry out his prayer life without fear or intimidation.

While he was praying and making supplication before God, those who plotted against him witnessed all he was doing. Daniel was protected by God, who closed the mouths of the lions and delivered him from death.

Daniel was given gifts that were not common to men, as dream interpretation and visions were part of his calling. Daniel sought the meaning of a vision he had been given, and God granted him understanding. Gabriel appeared to Daniel in the form of a man and explained the vision to Daniel. Daniel 8:15-16

Daniel was conversant with intercessory prayer, not only for himself but for the people. Daniel wrote the following which assists our understanding.

"Now while I was speaking, praying,
and confessing my sin and the sin of my people Israel,
and presenting my supplication before the Lord my God,
while I was speaking in prayer, the man Gabriel,
whom I had seen in the vision at the beginning,
being caused to fly swiftly,
reached me about the time of the evening offering."
Daniel 9:20-21

Daniel was accustomed to prayer and fasting when required. One time he wrote about what he saw as necessary for answered prayer and gaining spiritual knowledge.

> *"In those days, I, Daniel was mourning three full weeks.*
> *I ate no pleasant food,*
> *no meat or wine came into my mouth,*
> *nor did I anoint myself at all,*
> *till three whole weeks were fulfilled."*
>
> Daniel 10:2-3

Daniel was also aware of spiritual warfare as he prayed and fasted until the answer came. The delay was of little concern, for he knew God would provide him with the necessary information. Again, we read;

> *Then Gabriel said to me, "Do not fear, Daniel,*
> *for from the first day that you set your heart to understand,*
> *and to humble yourself before your God,*
> *your words were heard;*
> *and I have come because of your words.*
> *But the prince of the kingdom of Persia withstood me twenty-one days;*
> *and behold, Michael, one of the chief princes,*
> *came to help me,*
> *for I had been left alone there with the kings of Persia."*
>
> Daniel 10:12-13

Daniel was aware of the evil forces which plagued his life of prayer but he was persistent, patient, and persevered despite opposition to the revealed will of God as He revealed Himself to the heart of Daniel.

Eliezer. Genesis 24:12-14

Eliezer was the oldest and wisest servant who served Abraham. He was commissioned to find a suitable wife for his master's son, Isaac, from his people, not those in Canaan. Eliezer prayed to the God of his master for success, not to a God he personally knew. This would be the first prayer of agreement. It was Jesus who taught this concept before the Holy Spirit was given. Jesus promise to His hearers was;

> *"If any two of you agree on earth*
> *concerning anything that they ask,*
> *it will be done for them by My Father in heaven."*

Matthew 18:19

When Eliezer had made his petition to Father God, on behalf of another, his prayer was answered, for we are told;

> *"And it happened,*
> *before he had finished speaking, that behold,*
> *Rebekah came out with her pitcher on her shoulder."*

Genesis 24:15

Father God had not only heard the prayer of petition prayed by Eliezer but had answered before he had finished praying.

Elijah. 1 Kings 18:36-40

While Elijah had many talks with Father God, this is the only prayer recorded petitioning God to act. God acted because it was part of His plan to show His power and might to these wayward children, He chose to call His own.

Even though Elijah exhibited believing faith and was rewarded for his efforts, when faced with the fearsome Jezebel, his courage failed and he ran from her presence and hid. Decisions made always carry consequences, whether good or not so good.

Esther. 4:10-17

Although there is no prayer recorded in the Book of Esther, her actions speak louder than words, as she encouraged her people to follow her lead through fasting, and this they carried out. Fasting was seen by the Lord as a desperate people seeking His protection. This was what God had covenanted with Moses, what the people had agreed to, but so often disobedience followed. In Esther's prayer life, she recognized that she needed others to pray for her as fasting was always associated with prayer. Before Esther undertook the work the Lord had for her, she asked the entire city to fast and pray with her for 3 days. We need the strength that comes from the prayers of others to do the work the Lord has for us. God faithfully carried out His promise, by eventually eradicating those who dared to go against His people.

Ezekiel. 37:3a

Ezekiel is more well-known for his visions than he is for his prayer, as his prayer was in response to the Lord and His plans for the children of Israel. His words were;

"O Lord God,
You know."

Ezekiel knew God's plans for His people, but he felt inadequate to play his part. Ezekiel was told to prophesy and he obeyed. He spoke the words which were given to him, not his own words. When we speak the word of God, miracles happen.

Hannah. 1 Samuel 1:10-11

Hannah, Esther, Miriam, Deborah, Rebekah and Hagar are six women who prayed. Miriam and Deborah sang prayers of praise to the Lord God. Hagar's heart cried out silently and;

"God heard the voice of the lad.
Then the Angel of God called to Hagar from heaven
and said to her,
'What troubles you, Hagar?'"

Genesis 21:17a

Hannah was in a similar situation but was childless. She cried out silently to the Lord, but unlike Haggar, Hannah vowed to the Lord, a promise she covenanted to keep. Although she was seen as a drunken woman by Eli the priest, when she told Eli her petition, the priest acknowledged or agreed with Hannah as he said;

> *"Go in peace,*
> *and the God of Israel grant your petition*
> *which you have asked of Him."*
>
> 1 Samuel 1:17

God granted Hannah the petition from her heart, and she gave birth to a boy whom they called Samuel. In Hannah's petition to the Lord she vowed to, *"Give him to the Lord all the days of his life"* (1 Samuel 1:11b). When she eventually took Samuel and presented him to Eli, she said;

> *"For this child I prayed,*
> *and the Lord has granted me my petition*
> *which I asked of Him.*
> *Therefore I also have lent him to the Lord;*
> *as long as he lives he shall be lent to the Lord."*
>
> 1 Samuel 1:27-28

Hanna covenanted to *'give'* him to the Lord, but when the time came, she only *'lent'* him to the Lord. The one difference between Hannah and most of the others is that she followed up the granting of her petition with a prayer of thankfulness and gratefulness to the Lord for what He had completed in her life. 1 Samuel 2:1-10

Isaac. Genesis 25:21

There are no recorded prayers from Isaac, but we are told that he pleaded with the Lord for his wife and on her behalf. His petition was granted and his wife Rebekah became pregnant with twin boys.

Rebekah. Genesis 25:22

Just like her husband Isaac, there is no record of what Rebekah asked of the Lord. Her pregnancy was not as she had expected or was told to expect from other women. She was concerned with what was happening within herself as she knew something was different but had no idea what. After expressing her innermost thoughts, when she said, *"If all is well, why am I like this?"* Rebekah asked the Lord for an answer.

The Lord heard her plea and brought peace to a troubled soul. While the twins struggled within her, she trusted God for the fulfilment of what He had told her.

Jacob. Genesis 32:9-12, 24-32

Jacob is finally confronted with all the deceptions from his past life, but he earnestly cried out to the God of his father Abraham and Isaac for mercy, protection, deliverance and reminded God of His covenant with himself. Jacob continued to wrestle with the Man until daybreak and would not let go until he had secured a blessing. The Man continued;

> *"So He said to him, 'What is your name?'*
> *He said, 'Jacob'.*
> *And He said, 'Your name shall no longer be called Jacob,*
> *but Israel; for you have struggled with God and with men,*
> *and have prevailed'."*
>
> Genesis 32:27-28

Jehoshaphat. 2 Chronicles 20:6-12, 15-17

In the face of adversity, Jehoshaphat cried out to God for mercy and to protect His people from the enemy. He reminded God of the covenant secured with Abram so many years previous, to provide for them in their time of need. His petition was heard, as the Spirit of the Lord came upon Jahaziel, who spoke to the people of Israel the word of the Lord. The people were reassured that God was going before them, just as He did when their ancestors came out of Egypt, all they had to do was trust and not be afraid.

The message from the Spirit of the Lord said;

> *"Do not be afraid not dismayed*
> *because of this great multitude,*
> *for the battle is not yours, but God's."*
>
> 2 Chronicles 20:15b

The people believed the words of the Lord and sang praises to Him. God was true to His word, protected and rewarded His children for their courage and belief.

Job. 13:20-14:22, 40:4-5, 42:2-6

Job uttered three prayers. Although Job was blameless and an upright man, who shunned evil, he was self-righteous, but God required him to be God righteous. Job's confession was, *"I will defend my own ways before Him"* (Job 13:15). Elihu, the younger fourth friend commented, *"Job justified himself rather than God"* (Job 32:2). Job changed his confession in his final prayer when he said, *"I know that you can do anything, and that no purpose of Yours can be withheld from you."* Job 42:2

Jonah. 2:2-9

Spiritual persuasion is a tool used by Father God to good effect. Affliction was also present with Jonah in his distress. It would appear that there is nowhere or place where the ears of God do not hear a heartfelt plea. Jonah said;

> *"I cried out to the Lord because of my affliction,*
> *and He answered me.*
> *Out of the belly of Sheol I cried,*
> *and You heard my voice."*

Jonah 2:2

Jonah found that one situation led to another as he was still called by God to carry out what God had ordained. While God's grace covers our sin of rebellion, He requires us to be obedient to His revealed will for us each.

Joshua. 10:12a

Protection and mercy are often petitioned to Father God, especially when we are faced with what appears to be the impossible. What may seem like the craziest prayer, is always presented to Father God for His acceptance. Joshua knew that if the fighting ceased at sundown, there was a great possibility they would be defeated the next day. Father God examines our motives in all circumstances we find ourselves in, and then acts in accordance with His will.

This is the only prayer where *'the Lord heeded the voice of a man; for the Lord fought for Israel'*.

> *"Sun, stand still over Gibeon;*
> *and Moon, in the valley of Aijalon."*

> *"So the sun stood still,*
> *and the moon stopped,*
> *till the people had revenge*
> *upon their enemies."*
>
> Joshua 10:12a-13

Jeremiah. 20:7-18

Jeremiah was between a rock and a hard place. While he sincerely followed the Lord's command in obedience, he was hampered on every front, because of the persecution he endured. He desired to stop speaking in His name, but he could not. Although despondent, in Jeremiah's prayer, he reaches a high point of praise.

> *"Sing to the Lord! Praise the Lord!*
> *For He has delivered the life of the poor*
> *from the hand of the evildoers."*
>
> Jeremiah 20:13

Jeremiah, after the high point, once again sinks into the depths of despair. Caught between the divine call he cannot evade, and the rejection and persecution by the people, rejection by friends, he curses the day he was born.

King Hezekiah. 2 Kings 19:15-19

Hezekiah is an excellent illustration of what a believer should do when threatened by an enemy. Hezekiah does not react to the threats of Sennacherib but cries out to the Lord for Help.

> *"O Lord God of Israel,*
> *the One who dwells between the cherubim,*
> *You are God, You alone,*
> *of all the kingdoms of the earth.*
> *You have made heaven and earth.*
> *Incline Your ear, O Lord, and hear."*
>
> 2 Kings 19:15-16a

Because Sennacherib had dared challenge the One true God, He answered Hezekiah's request by going before them and slaying the entire Assyrian army.

> *"And it came to pass on a certain night*
> *that the angel of the Lord went out,*
> *and killed in the camp of the Assyrians*
> *one hundred and eighty-five thousand;*
> *and when people arose early in the morning,*
> *there were the corpses, all dead."*
>
> 2 Kings 19:35

Moses. Psalm 90

It appeared strange to find the prayer of Moses written and preserved in the Psalms. One could almost imagine Moses praying this prayer toward the end of their wanderings in the wilderness, as he had seen the mighty hand of God work against His enemies, and upon the wayward people He chose to call His own. Moses saw and experienced the wrath of God when leading the children of Israel out of captivity. How He dealt with those who were disobedient, but showed His grace to those who sought to follow Him.

Moses, in this prayer, petitions Father God to teach wisdom to future generations, to have compassion on them, and to satisfy them early with His mercy. Moses petitions the Lord to train up the future generations for he wrote;

> *"Make us glad according to the days*
> *in which You have afflicted us,*
> *the years in which we have seen evil.*
> *Let Your work appear to Your servants,*
> *and Your glory to their children.*
> *And let the beauty of the Lord our God be upon us,*
> *and establish the work of our hands for us;*
> *Yes, establish the work of our hands."*
>
> Psalm 90:15-17

Noah. Genesis 9:25-27

I am not going to speculate as to what had happened for this prayer of prophecy to be prayed by Noah. Ham showed no respect for his father and tried to coerce his brothers to do the same. Ham's son was also involved as the curse was directed at him. Ham himself became the father of the Canaanites, the Babylonians, the Phoenicians, the Cushites, and the Egyptians. Genesis 10:6-20

God gave directions to Moses (Deuteronomy 20:16-18), to utterly destroy all those who inhabited the *'Promised Land'*. Ham showed no respect for his father Noah. The Canaanites would do the same as they were cursed. They were to be destroyed so they would not persuade or corrupt the children of Israel. Ham tried to convince his brothers to look at their father with contempt as he did. But they showed reverence and walked backwards and covered him. God would later say;

> *"Honour your father and your mother,*
> *that your days may be long upon the land*
> *which the Lord your God is giving you."*
>
> Exodus 20:12

The children of Israel followed Ham's example and did not remain a separate people, totally disobedient to Father God. God will have His way eventually, eradicating all those who have not been redeemed by the blood of His Son, Jesus Christ. The chosen, the called will then inhabit the new promised land, containing the 'New Jerusalem', where we will worship our Heavenly Father in spirit and in truth.

Samson. Judges 16:28, 30

Samson was a Nazarite from his mother's womb until he died. His mission was to begin the freedom of the children of Israel from the oppression of the Philistines. As God supplied all his needs, one by one he disobeyed each requirement set down to his parents. After the cutting of his hair, which was the last, the presence of God departed. Enduring much torment, suffering and ridicule, Samson cried out to God in repentance, and God answered his prayer.

Solomon. 1 Kings 3:6-9

Solomon was never trained or prepared to become the successor to his father David. It was the prophet Nathan who saw the potential in Solomon and reminded his mother, Bathsheba, of the promise David had made to her many years previous that Solomon would take his place.

Solomon loved the Lord walking in the ways of his father David, but he sacrificed and burned incense at the high altar. At Gibeon the Lord appeared to Solomon in a dream by night; and God said, *"Ask! What shall I give you?"* Solomon replied to the Lord;

Betrayal

> *"Now, O Lord my God,*
> *You have made Your servant king instead of my father David,*
> *but I am a little child;*
> *I do not know how to go out or come in.*
>
> *Therefore give to Your servant an understanding heart*
> *to judge Your people,*
> *that I may discern between good and evil.*
> *For who is able to judge this great people of Yours?"*
>
> 1 Kings 3:7, 9

Father God was pleased with the answer given, that was petitioned to Him. He granted Solomon his request but so much more accompanied his wise choice.

People Who Prayed in the Old Testament.

Person	Prayer Purpose or Topic	Scripture Reference
Abraham	Interceded for Sodom	Genesis 18:16-33
Daniel	Prayed for the people	Daniel 9:1-19
David	Prayer was his life's foundation.	Various
Eliezer	Wisdom to choose a bride for Isaac	Genesis 24:12-14
Elijah	God to revealed Himself as the true God	1 Kings 18:36-40
Esther	Justice for God's people	Esther 4:10-17
Ezekiel	Answered the Lord's question	Ezekiel 37:3a
Hannah	A son born to her for God's use	1 Samuel 1:10
Isaac	Intercession for his wife Rebekah	Genesis 25:21
Jacob	Prayed for protection from Esau	Genesis 32:9-12
Jehoshaphat	Deliverance from their enemies	2 Chronicles 20:6-12
Job	The self-righteous to become righteous	Job 13:20-14:22. 40:4-5. 42:2-6
Jonah	Prayed for deliverance	Jonah 2:2-9
Joshua	Deliverance from their enemy	Joshua 10:12
Jeremiah	Prayed for himself and his unpopular ministry	Jeremiah 20:7-18
King Hezekiah	Overthrow Sennacherib for reproaching God	2 Kings 19:15-19
Moses	The eternity of God and man's frailty	Psalm 90
Noah	Blessing and cursing on his family	Genesis 9:25-27
Rebekah	Questioned her condition	Genesis 25:22
Samson	Prayer of repentance and renewed faith	Judges 16:28,30
Solomon	Prayed for an understanding heart	1 Kings 3:6-9

The Angel of the Lord Appearances

Old Testament. Abraham, Eliezer, Isaac, Jacob, Moses, Manoah, Joshua, Hannah, Daniel, King Hezekiah, Job, Esther, Jonah, Elijah, David, Noah, Ezekiel, Jehoshaphat, Rebekah, Solomon, Jeremiah, and Zechariah.

New Testament. Joseph, Rolled back the stone, Zacharias, Appearance to Shepherds, Opened prison doors, Appearance to Moses, Philip, Peter, and Herod.

The Angel of the Lord Appearances

Old Testament	Scripture	New Testament	Scripture
Abraham	Genesis 18:16-33	Joseph	Matthew 1:20-24
Daniel	Daniel 9:1-19	Flight into Egypt	Matthew 2:13-19
David	Psalm 86 and 51	Rolled back the stone	Matthew 28:2
David	1 Chronicles 21:15	Zacharias	Luke 1:11
Eliezer	Genesis 24:12-14	Appeared to the shepherds	Luke 2:9
Elijah	1 Kings 18:36-40	Opened prison doors	Acts 5:19
Esther	Esther 4:10-17	Appeared to Moses	Acts 7:30
Ezekiel	Ezekiel 36:26	Philip	Acts 8:26
Hannah	1 Samuel 1:10	Peter released from prison	Acts 12:7, v5 - v19
King Hezekiah	2 Kings 19:15-19	Herod	Acts 12:23
Isaac	Genesis 25:21		
Jacob	Genesis 32:9-12		
Jehoshaphat	2 Chronicles 20:6-12, 15-17		
Jeremiah	Jeremiah 20:7-18		
Job	Job 13:21		
Jonah	Jonah 2:2-9		
Joshua	Joshua 10:12a		
Moses	Psalm 90		
Manoah	Judges 13:3		
Noah	Genesis 10:3-7		
Rebekah	Genesis 25:2		
Solomon	1 Kings 3:6-9		
Zechariah	Zechariah chap.1-6,12		

David's Life of Prayer.

Unlike people who have one or two prayers recorded in the Old Testament, David has at least nineteen prayers not including songs, accredited to him. Six of the prayers are associated with Saul and his dealing with David, one is used in regular worship, one prayer deals with David's confession, two deal with administrating justice and nine have to do with other times when David shared a prayer, but not placed with an event.

All of David's prayers can be found in the Psalms, 1st and 2nd Samuel, and 1st Chronicles. Following David's progression from a young shepherd to an aged King, demonstrates his spiritual growth, through his prayers, or in some cases, spiritual decline.

Although the Twenty-third Psalm is not a prayer as such, it is the foundation on which David established his whole life. As the psalm is the testimony to his belief, security and trust in Father God, this gave David an understanding that most of the people did not have.

Using the 23rd Psalm as his foundation, David's remaining Psalms follow in the sequence of his life. Psalm 56, Psalm 57, Psalm 142, Psalm 54, Psalm 39, Psalm 51, Psalm 3, Psalm 7, Psalm 60, Psalm 5, Psalm 6, Psalm 9, Psalm 17, Psalm 26, Psalm 38, Psalm 70, Psalm 86, and lastly Psalm 141.

David's Ancestry.

Salmon, from the tribe of Judah, married Rahab, the high priestess of Asherah. A son was born to them whom they called Boaz. Boaz married Ruth, the daughter-in-law of Naomi, also of the tribe of Judah. Boaz and Ruth had a son whom they called Obed. Obed's wife had a son whom they called Jesse. David was the great, great-grandson of Salmon and the great-grandson of Boaz, all in the bloodline of the tribe of Judah.

David was the youngest of eight sons born to Jesse, the Bethlehemite. Eliab is David's oldest brother (1 Samuel 16:6; 17:13, v28; 1 Chronicles 2:13). The second born is Abinadab (1 Samuel 16:8; 17:13; 1 Chronicles 2:13).

David's third oldest brother is Shimea (1 Samuel 16:9; 1 Chronicles 2:13). Shimea is alternately spelled Shammah (1 Samuel 17:13) and Shimeah (2 Samuel 13:3). The fourth brother is Nethanel, the fifth Raddai, and the sixth Ozem (1 Chronicles 2:14-15). Chronicles also names two sisters of David: Zeruiah and Abigail (1 Chronicles 2:16). However, two brothers are missing from this list of names, and presumed they had died before fathering any children.

While there is dispute over the number of sons, either seven or eight, the account of David's anointing informs us,

> *"Thus Jesse made seven of his sons pass before Samuel.*
> *And Samuel said to Jessie, 'The Lord has not chosen these.*
> *Are all the young men here?'*
> *Then he said, 'There remains yet the youngest,*
> *and there he is, keeping the sheep.'*
> *And Samuel said to Jesse, 'Send and bring him.*
> *For we will not sit down till he comes here'."*
>
> 1 Samuel 16:10-11

David was looking after the flock of sheep near the home, as Jesse pointed him out to Samuel. David was left to tend the flocks when the prophet Samuel consecrated seven of Jesse's sons and invited them to the sacrifice (1 Samuel 16:5). God had told Samuel He would choose one of the sons to be anointed king, but the family never considered David as a possibility. 1 Samuel 16:11

Betrayal

Samuel was not aware of David's existence as he would have chosen Eliab, David's eldest brother as the one to be anointed. When Samuel inquired of the Lord, he was told;

> *"Do not look at his appearance*
> *or at his physical stature,*
> *because I have refused him.*
> *For the Lord does not see as man sees;*
> *for man looks at the outward appearance,*
> *but the Lord looks at the heart."*
>
> 1 Samuel 16:7

According to Jewish tradition, David's mother was Nitzevet, the wife of Jesse. Jesse, began to doubt the purity of his ancestry, since he was the great-grandson of Rahab, the high priestess of Asherah, and grandson of Ruth the Moabitess (Ruth 4:17). Due to his doubts, having seven sons to Nitzevet, Jesse planned to marry his Canaanite servant and have children with her. The maidservant pitied Nitzevet and offered Nitzevet a plan. On the wedding night, Nitzevet and the maidservant could secretly switch places, as Leah and Rachael's switch had deceived Jacob.

When Nitzevet became pregnant with David, her eighth son, she never revealed to Jesse what she had done, even when her pregnancy was apparent. Nitzevet came to be despised as an immoral woman, and her son, David, grew up an outcast in his own family. David would write later two verses that could relate to this situation;

> *"Behold, I was brought forth in inequity,*
> *and in sin my mother conceived me."*
>
> Psalm 51:6

> *"I have become a stranger to my brothers,*
> *and an alien to my mother's children."*
>
> Psalm 69:8

While this fact is believed in Jewish tradition, it is not recorded in the Bible and therefore can't be substantiated as truth, but it is a possibility.

David was different to the other children as he played the harp, wrote poetry and possibly sang as he spent much time outdoors with the sheep in his father's pasture. He had an understanding and a caring heart for nature and the God of creation.

As it is thought Psalm 23 was written when David was tending his father's flock, a reference to the possible prayer placement, will be considered as a response to how the prayer impacted David personally, and King Saul.

Psalm 23. 1 Samuel 16:14-23

King Saul had disobeyed the Lord who had removed His Spirit from him and another spirit graced the innermost part of King Saul.

> *"But the Spirit of the Lord departed from Saul,*
> *and a distressing spirit from the Lord troubled him."*
>
> 1 Samuel 16:14

David's journey with Saul began when one of Saul's unnamed servants recommended David play the harp to him. The unnamed servant said;

> *"Look, I have seen a son of Jesse the Bethlehemite,*
> *who is skilful in playing, a mighty man of valour,*
> *a man of war, prudent in speech,*
> *and a hansom person;*
> *and the Lord is with him."*
>
> 1 Samuel 16:18

The fact that a stranger gave this report about David to King Saul, says a lot about the shepherd boy David and his upbringing. David was close to his mother and the care she displayed to him and taught him the ways of Father God. On one occasion, he pays tribute to his godly mother when he wrote;

David's Life of Prayer.

> *"Oh, turn to me,*
> *and have mercy on me!*
> *Give Your strength to Your servant,*
> *and save the son of Your maidservant."*

Psalm 86:16

When Saul was troubled, David would play his harp and Saul would be at ease. Saul was an anointed person and knew the presence of the Holy Spirit, but now a different spirit occupied his soul.

As David, sat in the open field tending his flock of sheep, he saw the parallel between everything he had seen and done with the Creator and the God he knew. What better spiritual calm would be created than the words of his psalm to soothe the soul. David expressed his thoughts with the following words which would allow the distressed soul to be calmed.

> *The Lord is my shepherd;*
> *I shall not want.*
> *He makes me to lie down in green pastures;*
> *He leads me beside the still waters.*
> *He restores my soul.*

Psalm 23:1-3a

Even when David resided in Saul's house, he would occasionally go and feed his father's sheep in Bethlehem. The three eldest brothers had joined the armed service of Saul. As a father, Jesse would have been concerned for the safety of all his sons and chose to send David with some supplies to them, so he could report back with positive news.

When David arrived at the battle site, he greeted his brothers. While David was speaking with some of the other men, Goliath, the uncircumcised champion of the Philistines came up and defied the armies of the living God. David made inquiries about the rewards for delivering Israel from this giant of a man. Eliab, his oldest brother became angry with David, for he said;

> *"Why did you come down here?*
> *And with whom have you left*
> *those few sheep in the wilderness?*
> *I know your pride and the insolence of your heart,*
> *for you have come down to see the battle."*
>
> 1 Samuel 17:28

David replied;

> *"What have I done now?*
> *Is there not a cause?"*

1 Samuel 17:29

Eliab was embarrassed that David had witnessed the real battle. He tried to embarrass his little brother in front of the fighting men, but the Spirit of God within him spoke and reproved Eliab in front of them all. What had proceeded from the mouth of David was conveyed to King Saul.

When David stood before the King, he was unaware of David's history. Saul saw a young man playing his harp which brought comfort to his stressful state, not a man of God to be reckoned with. He hadn't even enquired about his background, where he was from or about his exploits. Saul was so consumed with his importance, why would he care about others, besides, he was the reigning King.

When David shared with him how he had protected his father's flock of sheep from a bear and a lion, Saul knew this youth had an inner strength that was missing in his life. Saul was not prepared to meet Goliath in battle, but David was unafraid. Saul gave David his armour, a bronze helmet, clothed him with a coat of mail and fastened his sword to his armour.

What had King Saul just done? Positions of authority were marked by special clothing. Even more important, the ruler's weapon, usually a sword, was seen as the mark of their favour to the bearer as the legitimate ruler. In Israelite culture, Saul was offering David his position as king of Israel. As the sword was seen as the defender of Israel, kingship accompanied this act.

By returning the armour and sword that had been given to Him, David showed that he did not intend to replace Saul as King as David knew, he was not ready to rule. He held to this position firmly, even later avoiding confrontation with Saul. David knew it was God's timing that was important, not his own perceived desires. David did not rely on the physical protection provided to him because he knew the protection of God was all he required.

David left Saul's presence and went to the brook where he selected five smooth stones and placed them in his shepherd's bag. When he went to face Goliath, he was met with scorn and abuse. In return, David prophesied over Goliath about his death. 1 Samuel 17:45-47

"When Saul saw David going out against the Philistine, he said to Abner, the commander of the army, 'Abner, whose son is this youth?' And Abner said, 'As your soul lives, O king, I do not know.' So the king said, 'Inquire whose son this young man is'." 1 Samuel 17:55-56

David is now recognised for who he is. He's not just a harp player but the champion, a national hero of all Israel. Saul and David spoke at some length after the victory, while Jonathan, Saul's son and heir, who should succeed his father, took off the robe he was wearing, and gave it, along with his armour, sword, bow and belt to David. Just as Saul had offered his sword and armour, and the surrender of his kingdom, Jonathan recognised in David, that the Spirit of the living God dwelt in him. He surrendered all claim to the throne that rightfully was his.

David accompanied Saul wherever he went and was accepted everywhere they travelled. The women came out and sang the praises of both but with a difference. They saw David as one who achieved more than the king, which made Saul angry with David.

Psalm 56. 1 Samuel 21:10-15

Saul resented David for his popularity and became very jealous to the point, that Saul wanted David dead. How quickly life had changed for David. Saul told Jonathan and all his servants, that they should kill David. When his son Jonathan suggested that Saul would be transgressing God with innocent blood, Saul relented and David once again returned to his wife Michal and his home.

Saul was again afflicted with the distressing spirit, so David was called and he played his harp. As David realised Saul was going to kill him with a spear near him, he made his escape, but Saul sent messengers to David's house to kill David in the morning. When Michal heard, she told David and let him down through a window and placed an image in the bed. When Saul discovered what his daughter had done, she replied, *"He said to me, 'Let me go! Why should I kill you?'"* 1 Samuel 19:17b

David went from participating in the king's court and living a life with his loved wife to the life of a fugitive. But with everything that happened, David always remained faithful to Father God and always sought His advice on how he should act and proceed. Samuel remained a stanched ally who had supported David from his anointing so, David met him at Ramah where he knew he was safe.

David couldn't understand why his father-in-law would want to kill him. He contacted Jonathan who once again swore loyalty to David. Because Jonathan knew his father hid nothing from him, he promised to keep David informed. Jonathan devised a plan so David would know Saul's mood. David was to hide in a predetermined field where Johnathan would practice his archery skills with a young lad. Depending on the command he gave to the boy, David would know if it was safe to return or flee.

When David was missed from the new moon feast, Saul accused Jonathan of being the son of a perverse, rebellious woman. When Jonathan questioned his father Saul about the reason, he cast a spear at Jonathan to kill him, so Jonathan left to warn David of the impending death threat.

When Johnathan and David were alone in the field, Jonathan said to David;

> "Go in peace,
> since we have both sworn
> in the name of the Lord, saying,
> 'May the Lord be between you and me,
> and between your descendants
> and my descendants, forever'."
>
> 1 Samuel 20:42b

David arrived at Nob where he conversed with the priest Ahimelech but swore him to secrecy. David acquired some old holy bread and Goliath's sword because David was unarmed. But his presence had been noticed by one of Saul's herdsmen by the name of Doeg.

David left and fled to Gath, the place where Goliath and his family lived, but when he realised this was not a good place to be, he prayed for relief from tormentors.

> *"Be merciful to me, O God,*
> *for man would swallow me up;*
> *fighting all day he oppresses me.*
> *My enemies would hound me all day,*
> *for there are many who fight against me,*
> *O Most High."*

> *"Vows made to You are binding upon me, O God;*
> *I render praises to You.*
> *For You have delivered my soul from death,*
> *have You not kept my feet from falling,*
> *that I may walk before God in the light of the living."*
>
> Psalm 56:1-2, 12-13.

Psalm 57. 1 Samuel 24:1-22.

David fled to the desert and found refuge in the cave of Adullam. When David's family heard where David was, they packed up and went to join him, along with many others. David was able to form an army of about four hundred men so he went to the king of Moab, the home of his ancestors, Rahab and Ruth, and inquired of the king if his father and mother could live there under his protection which was granted.

The prophet Gad told David to depart the stronghold of Moab and along with his men, go to Judah. When Saul heard of the different places David had travelled through, he led his army in pursuit. But just at a crucial time for David and his men, word came to Saul about the Philistines invading his land so, Saul returned to wage war with the Philistines. They called the place the 'Rock of Escape', and then David and his men travelled to the strongholds of En Gedi.

When Saul was told that David had been seen in the Wilderness of En Gedi, he took three thousand chosen men to seek out David. When David arrived at a cave, he prayed to Father God. The following is part of the prayer he offered.

"Be merciful to me, O God,
be merciful to me!
For my soul trusts in You;
and in the shadow of Your wings
I will make my refuge,
until these calamities have passed by."

"I will praise You, O Lord,
among the peoples;
I will sing to You among the nations;
for Your mercy reaches unto the heavens,

and Your truth unto the clouds.
Be exalted, O God,
above the heavens;
Let Your glory be above all the earth."

Psalm 57:1, 9-11

As David and his men settled into the cave, David made a further petition to Father God.

Psalm 142.
"I cry out to the Lord with my voice;
with my voice to the Lord I make my supplication.
I pour out my complaint before Him;
I declare before Him my trouble.

Bring my soul out of prison,
that I may praise Your name;
the righteous shall surround me,
for You shall deal bountifully with me."

Psalm 142:1, 7

Saul found the cave but did not know David and his men were hiding in the back part. He entered and laid down to rest. The men encouraged David to kill Saul, but David would not lift his hand against the Lord's anointed, instead, he cut off the corner of Saul's robe.

When Saul had re-joined his men, David called out to Saul and showed him the corner of his robe. Saul was convicted in his heart, realising David would succeed him to be the next king of Israel so he replied to David;

> *"You are more righteous than I;*
> *for you have rewarded me with good,*
> *whereas I have rewarded you with evil."*
>
> 1 Samuel 24:17

Saul returned home, and David went his way. David was blameless in all his ways and thoughts as he did not repay evil for evil, but sought to fulfil what was his reasonable service to Father God. David always remained open to God and his dealing with those who sought to do him harm.

David had dramatic changes to deal with during his life. One could imagine David at times, wondered whether his being the King of Israel would ever come to pass, as he had been anointed by Samuel. He never sought to do King Saul harm but always acted with complete respect to him as he was the Lord's anointed. Samuel had died and David was a fugitive. How could anything come to pass?

David was told of a businessman in Carmel who may help them with supplies. Nabal was a very rich man but did not recognise David or his men's needs. Nabal was harsh and evil in his business dealings, but his wife Abigail was of good understanding and beautiful appearance. Nabal refused to help in any way, shape or form, but Abigail was informed by some of her workers how David and his men had protected them.

David was about to massacre Nabal and his business when he met Abigail who had provisions for them. She talked at length with David and apologised for her husband. David accepted her kind words and withheld his hand against them. Abigail waited for an opportune time to tell her husband what she had done, and when she did, his heart died within him, and he became like a stone. After about ten days, Nabal died.

When David heard of Nabal's death, he sent servants to Abigail with a marriage proposal to become his wife, which she willingly accepted.

David was careful to remember how the Lord had answered his prayers. His prayer of thankfulness for his deliverance and protection was petitioned to Father God.

Psalm 54.
> *"Save me, O God, by Your name,*
> *and vindicate me by Your strength.*

David's Life of Prayer.

Hear my prayer, O God;
give ear to the words of my mouth.

For He has delivered me out of all trouble;
and my eye has seen its desire upon my enemies."

Psalm 54:1-2, 7.

It should be noted, that in most things, David sought the direction of the Lord. Unlike Saul, from whom the Spirit of God had departed, who sought revenge on David whom he knew was God's anointed and would be his successor. The Ziphites came to Saul at Gibeah and told him that David was hiding in the hill of Hachilah so Saul, with three thousand chosen men who accompanied him, encamped on the hill of Hachilah.

When night came, David and Abishai, the son of Zeruiah, brother of Joab, went to Saul's campsite. There was Saul, in the middle of the camp, Abner his chief commander next to him, all sound asleep. They silently made their way through the sleeping soldiers and stood next to Saul. Abishai wanted to spear Saul to the ground with Saul's spear which was next to him, but David would not lift his hand against the Lord's anointed.

Again, the Lord went before David and Abishai and cast a deep sleep over all the soldiers including Saul so David took

Saul's spear and water jug, which was next to Saul's head and left. Nobody was aware that anyone had entered the camp, let alone stood next to the king and his chief commander.

When morning came, David stood on top of a distant hill and called to Abner and told him he should die, because he had not protected the king from intruders. When Saul heard David's voice he said, *"Is that your voice, my son David?"* David answered and said;

> *"Here is the king's spear.*
> *Let one of the young men come over and get it.*
> *For the Lord delivered you into my hand today,*
> *but I would not stretch out my hand*
> *against the Lord's anointed."*
>
> 1 Samuel 26:23

> *"Then Saul said to David,*
> *'May you be blessed, my son David!*
> *You shall both do great things and also still prevail'."*
>
> 1 Samuel 26:25

Saul found grace in the eyes of David when he spared his life a second time. So, David went his way, and Saul returned to his palace.

David thought he would find refuge in the land of the Philistines, as Saul would not dare to attack him there so, David with his six hundred men and their households came to Achish the son of Maoch, king of Gath. David asked for an area to be their own and was given Ziglag. David attacked many areas in the southern part of Judah and reported his fighting and measures to Achish.

There came a day when the Philistines gathered together to wage war against Israel so, David and his men paraded behind the Philistine armies. When the princes saw David and his men, they inquired as to why they were with them as they were Hebrews. Achish said in their defence;

> *"Is this not David,*
> *the servant of Saul king of Israel,*
> *who has been with me these days,*
> *or these years?*
> *And to this day I have found no fault in him*
> *since he defected to me."*
>
> 1 Samuel 29:3b

Although Achish tried his best to convince the princes, David was told to leave early the next morning, before the battle began, which he did and returned to Ziglag with his men.

Betrayal

While David and his men had been away from their camp, the Amalekites had raided, burnt their dwellings and carried away all the spoils including the people. When they arrived at the smouldering remains, David was in danger of being stoned, but *"David strengthened himself in the Lord his God."* 1 Samuel 30:6b

David inquired of the Lord, what course of action he should take and as a favourable reply was given, David and his men pursued the enemy. Along the way, they found a young Egyptian servant boy sick, who had been left by his master. They cared for the servant, who led them to the camp of the raiders. David and his men attacked killing all except four hundred who escaped on camels. David and his men rescued their families and retrieved all their possessions including additional spoil to take back to Ziglag.

David was accustomed to battle and death, but when the news that Saul and his three sons had died, David mourned for them all, especially the Lord's anointed, King Saul. A man came from Saul's camp with his clothes torn and dust on his head and prostrated himself in front of David and he told how he had found Saul leaning on his spear, weary and not able to continue. Saul instructed the man to kill him which he did. David then tore his clothes, as did all the men with him.

David's Life of Prayer.

> *"And they mourned and wept and fasted*
> *until evening for Saul and for Jonathan his son,*
> *for the people of the Lord and for the house of Israel,*
> *because they had fallen by the sword."*
>
> 2 Samuel 1:12

After this, David called the man to himself and enquired about Saul's death, and why it was that he was not afraid to put forth his hand to destroy the Lord's anointed? Then David called one of the young men and said;

> *"Go near, and execute him!*
> *And he struck him so that he died.*
> *So David said to him,*
> *'Your blood is on your own head,*
> *for your own mouth has testified against you',*
> *saying, 'I have killed the Lord's anointed'."*
>
> 1 Samuel 1:14b

God had opened the way for David, as he was anointed, and became the King of Judah.

After the death of King Saul, David sought the Lord's advice and the Lord told him to go up to Hebron. David obediently followed what the Lord had told him, and all the contingent of David settled in Hebron.

> *"Then the men of Judah came,*
> *and there they anointed David king*
> *over the house of Judah."*
>
> 2 Samuel 2:4a

Abner, the commander of Saul's army, took Ishbosheth, the son of Saul to reign over Israel. Only the house of Judah followed David. Israel and Judah were now at war. David's commander Joab, and Abner met to do battle, but Joab's soldiers overcame many of Abner's soldiers until both returned to their respective places. The war between the house of David and the house of Saul was long, but David grew stronger and the house of Saul grew weaker and weaker.

Abner, who was a force to be reckoned with came and allied with David so that David would be established as the King of Israel and take the place of King Saul. Abner was murdered due to a misunderstanding by one of David's army personnel. David was unaware that Joab, his nephew, had killed Abner out of revenge.

After the death of Abner, two of Saul's captains, murdered Ishbosheth at noon as he lay in his bed. They were held accountable for their actions and executed at the command of David. Only Father God could have designed such a path from the anointing of the shepherd boy David, to the anointed King of Israel.

All the tribes of Israel came to David at Hebron and spoke, saying;

"Indeed we are your bone and your flesh.
In time past, when Saul was king over us,
you were the one who led Israel out and brought them in;
and the Lord said to you,
'You shall shepherd My people Israel,
and be ruler over Israel'."

2 Samuel 5:2

King David made a covenant with them at Hebron before the Lord and they anointed David king of Israel. David went to Jerusalem and took possession from the Jebusites who thought they were invincible because of where their stronghold was situated. David's men climbed up the internal water shaft and defeated the Jebusites from within. David called the city the *'City of David'*.

When the Philistines heard that David was the anointed king over Israel, they declared war. David sought guidance from the Lord so when the Lord told him to go, he went.

Twice David confronted the Philistine armies, and twice they were defeated. The fame of David went out into all lands, and the Lord brought the fear of him upon all nations.

The Ark of the Covenant was to be brought up to Jerusalem and placed in the Tabernacle which David had erected. He obtained a new cart and placed the Ark in the back. But as they travelled, the oxen stumbled and Uzzah took hold of the Ark to steady it and was instantly struck dead for his error. David left the Ark in the house of Obed-Edom.

After three months, David aware of his error, rectified the situation as he had not carried out the requirement set by Father God for when the Ark was to be moved. David addressed the people of Jerusalem and said;

> *"No one may carry the ark of God but the Levites,*
> *for the Lord has chosen them to carry the ark of God*
> *and to minister before Him forever."*
>
> 1 Chronicles 15:2

David was clothed with a robe of fine linen, as were the Levites who bore the ark, the singers, and Chenaniah the music master but David also wore a linen ephod. There was much singing, playing and celebration, and David danced before the Lord. When the ark of the covenant of the Lord came to the City of David, Michal, Saul's daughter, looked through the window and saw King David whirling and playing music, and she despised him in her heart.

Michal was David's first wife given to him by Saul, but when Saul was pursuing David, he gave her to Palti the son of Laish, to block David from claiming the kingship through her.

Michal ridiculed David for his outburst in front of his people so David replied to Michal;

> "It was before the Lord,
> who chose me instead of your father and all his house,
> to appoint me ruler over the people of the Lord,
> over Israel.
> Therefore I will play music before the Lord.
> And I will be more undignified than this,
> and will be humble in my own sight."
>
> 2 Samuel 6:21-22a

Because she was disrespectful to the Lord's anointed, Michal the daughter of Saul had no more children to the day of her death.

Psalm 39. 1 Chronicles 16:37-43.
As the anointed King of Judah, David was able to establish regular worship services. Prayer was an essential

part of worship and one of David's prayers is included in the Psalms. The prayer for wisdom and forgiveness.

I said, "I will guard my ways,
lest I sin with my tongue;
I will restrain my mouth with a muzzle,
while the wicked are before me.
I was mute with silence,
I held my peace even from good;
and my sorrow was stirred up.
My heart was hot within me;
while I was musing, the fire burned.
Then I spoke with my tongue.

Hear my prayer, O Lord,
and give ear to my cry;
Do not be silent at my tears;
for I am a stranger with You,
a sojourner, as all my fathers were.
Remove Your gaze from me,
that I may regain strength,
before I go away and am no more."

Psalm 39:1-3, 12-13

Father God had completed the anointing process and installed David as King of Israel. David led other conflicts between the ancient tribes of Noah's descendants. The prophet Nathan had taken the place of Samuel. As King David lived in a house made of cedar, he thought it only right that the *'Temple of God'* should be better. When David told his intentions to Nathan, his response was;

> *"Do all that is in your heart,*
> *for God is with you."*
>
> 1 Chronicles 17:2

The prophet Nathan received word from Father God, dealing with this matter that King David had raised. Nathen revealed to David, that while his intentions were admirable, the building of God's temple was reserved for another. David's response was to pray to the Lord God and his reply can be found in 1 Chronicles 17:16 to 27.

David had covenanted with Jonathan, Saul's son to remain faithful to his family so, David inquired as to any living relative of Jonathan. One of Saul's servants remembered Jonathan's son by the name of Mephibosheth. When his father was killed, fearing that the Philistines would seek his life, the nurse fled with him to Gibeah, the royal residence, but in her haste, she dropped him and both his feet were crippled. 2 Samuel 4:4

David sent for the young man so he could show kindness to him for his father Jonathan's sake. When Mephibosheth came before David he prostrated himself before the king, saying, "Here is your servant!" David replied;

"Do not fear,
for I will surely show you kindness
for Jonathan your father's sake,
and will restore to you all the land
of Saul your grandfather;
and you shall eat bread at my table continually."

2 Samuel 9:7

Then he bowed himself, and said,
"What is your servant,
that you should look upon such a dead dog as I?"

2 Samuel 9:8

When Mephibosheth called himself a 'dead dog', he was reducing himself to the lowest possible realm. As a verbal sign of humility, Mephibosheth couldn't have said more to King David to show the difference in their positions. David was the king, while Mephibosheth, Saul's grandson, was a dead dog. David was true to his word and Mephibosheth was treated as one of royal descent.

But there came a time when David stayed home instead of leading his men into battle. There is a saying, 'The devil finds work for idle hands'. It would appear, although nothing is recorded, that David didn't ask the Lord for direction. One could imagine he thought he had fulfilled the known will of God as He revealed Himself to his heart.

Psalm 51. 2 Samuel 12:1-15

There was a time when David focused his whole life on God and did what God expected of him as the chosen and anointed leader of Israel. One would find it hard to understand the mindset of David, from a lowly shepherd boy to the ruler of Israel as He was invincible when the power of God went before him in everything he did. God favoured him, but he was about to enter the darkest time in his life.

As David strolled on his balcony, he saw a beautiful woman bathing and his heart lusted for her. Although she was married, he took her to himself and she consented. She became pregnant which complicated their situation. According to the law, they both should be stoned for committing adultery, but David formulated a plan of action to cover the increasing sin.

He sent for her husband who was one of his fighting men. Uriah did not sleep with Bathsheba but slept in the soldier's quarters as he would not indulge in pleasures while the battle raged. Frustrated, David sent a letter to Joab, his nephew, the commander of his army, to send Uriah into the heat of the battle and then withdraw. Uriah was killed.

Nathan the prophet confronted King David and told him a parable. When David became enraged about the actions of the people in the parable, Nathan said,

> *"You are the man."*
>
> 2 Samuel 12:7a

Nathan outlined exactly what David had done to his shame and horror. David accepted what Nathan had told him and repented. David's response was;

> *"I have sinned against the Lord."*
>
> 2 Samuel 12:13a

Nathan responded to David and said;

> *"The Lord also has put away your sin;*
> *you shall not die.*
> *However, because by this deed*
> *you have given great occasion to the enemies*

> *of the Lord to blaspheme,*
> *the child also who is born to you shall surely die."*
>
> 2 Samuel 12:14

What had happened to David who previously prayed positively to Father God, about his standing; upright and blameless? David had said in his prayer of praise,

> *"For all His judgments were before me;*
> *and as for His statutes,*
> *I did not depart from them.*
> *I was also blameless before Him,*
> *and I kept myself from my inequity."*
>
> 2 Samuel 22:23-24

David had witnessed his father-in-law's fall from grace and David did not want to experience his fate, but unlike Saul, David repented of his sin.

> *"Have mercy upon me, O God,*
> *according to Your lovingkindness;*
> *according to the multitude of Your tender mercies.*
> *Blot out my transgressions.*

Create in me a clean heart, O God,
and renew a steadfast spirit.
Do not take Your Holy Spirit from me.
Restore to me the joy of Your salvation,
and uphold me by Your generous Spirit.
Then I will teach transgressors Your ways,
and sinners shall be converted to You."

Psalm 51:1-2, 10-13

Psalm 3. 2 Samuel 15:1-37.

David was relieved that the Holy Spirit had not been taken away from him. He once again, relied on God for direction and protection. After the death of the baby, David and Bathsheba had four more sons, one they named Solomon. While David spent much time governing the Israelites, his family suffered. David's daughter Tamar was raped by her brother Amnon. Absalom, the older brother eventually killed Amnon and went into exile.

Wars were being fought and won with other nations, but the biggest threat was from his son Absalom, after David had forgiven him for instigating the murder of his brother, Absalom challenged his father David for his kingship. But David escaped from Jerusalem via the Kidron Brook and ascended the Mount of Olives and into the wilderness.

As David fled Jerusalem, he sent the *'Ark of the Covenant'* back into the city as He was convinced that if God favoured his cause, he would return and see it again.

> *"Lord, how they have increased who trouble me!*
> *Many are they who rise up against me.*
> *Many are they who say of me,*
> *'There is no help for him in God.'*
> *But You, O Lord, are a shield for me,*
> *my glory and the One who lifts up my head."*

> *"Arise, O Lord; save me, O my God!*
> *For You have struck all my enemies on the cheekbone;*
> *You have broken the teeth of the ungodly.*
> *Salvation belongs to the Lord.*
> *Your blessing is upon Your people."*
>
> Psalm 3:1-3, 7-8

Psalm 7. 2 Samuel 16:1-14.

While David is making his escape, he was met by two people with two different agendas. The first, Ziba, the servant of Mephibosheth offered a couple of saddled donkeys for the king's household to ride and rations for all the young men to eat. The other man was Shimei, who was from the house of Saul, who cursed and threw stones at David and his followers.

One of David's soldiers Abishai, wanted to cut off Shimei's head, but David restrained him saying;

> *"Let him alone, and let him curse;*
> *for so the Lord has ordered him.*
> *It may be that the Lord will look on my affliction,*
> *and that the Lord will repay me with good*
> *for his cursing this day."*
>
> 2 Samuel 16:11a-12

David understood only God could deliver them from the calamity his son had created so David sought the Lord in prayer for deliverance from their enemies.

> *"O Lord my God, in You I put my trust;*
> *Save me from all those who persecute me;*
> *and deliver me, lest they tear me like a lion,*
> *rending me in pieces,*
> *while there is none to deliver."*

> *"I will praise the Lord according to His righteousness,*
> *and will sing praise to the name of the Lord Most High."*
>
> Psalm 7:1-2, 17

Psalm 60. 1 Chronicles 18:14 to 20:8

David had come to realise that Father God had everything in control, even if at times he wondered how events would go in his favour. God used Hushai to warn the priests, Zadok and Abiathar to send a message via a servant girl to the house of her master where Jonathan and Ahimaaz were staying. Aware that the two had been seen, she hid them in the well, covered the entrance, and spread ground grain over the cover.

When Absalom's servants searched and could not find them, the servant girl told them that they had crossed over the brook, so they returned to Jerusalem. Jonathan and Ahimaaz warned King David not to camp in the wilderness but to cross over the Jordan, which they did.

Before both armies met to fight, King David gave the order to capture Absalom alive. As the battle took place in the fields and the woods, Absalom's army was defeated and David's men saw Absolom fleeing, riding on a mule. As the mule passed under a great terebinth tree, Absalom's head became wedged in the tree, and he was left hanging between heaven and earth.

The question could be asked, "Why did Absalom not get himself down and escape?" Absalom chose to ride on a mule, which was an animal reserved for a king. When the animal went under the tree, Absalom's head became wedged firmly in the fork of two branches. The impact on the neck possibly severed the spinal cord, and so rendered the rest of his body lifeless, dangling helplessly. He would not be able to lift his arms to free himself.

When Joab, the commander of David's army was told, he took three spears and thrust them through Absalom's heart. When David was told of his son's death, he mourned for him but Joab talked sternly to David about his actions, as they did not reflect his true concern for the people he ruled.

David was required to deal with Sheba's rebellion so he sent Joab to deal with the fugitive Sheba who was finally tracked down in Abel of Beth Maachah. When Joab's troops were battering down the wall, a wise woman asked to speak to Joab. When Joab told the woman they were seeking Sheba, she threw his head over the wall to Joab so Joab and his armies returned to Jerusalem.

Israel was in famine for three years so David questioned the Lord, and He revealed that Saul's transgression had caused the famine. It was revealed that Saul and his bloodthirsty house had killed the Gibeonites who were under the protection of the Amorites.

David agreed to atone for the wrongs caused by Saul and made an agreement with the Gibeonites who required seven men, descendants of the house of Saul, to be delivered to them for hanging. David agreed and chose Armoni and Mephibosheth, not the son of Jonathan, the two sons of Rizpah the daughter of Aiah, whom she bore to Saul, and the five sons of Michal, the daughter of Saul.

> *"So they fell, all seven together,*
> *and were put to death in the days of harvest,*
> *in the first days,*
> *in the beginning of barley harvest."*
>
> 2 Samuel 2:19b

The Philistines again brought war against Israel but, during the fighting, King David grew faint. Ishbi-Benob, who was one of the sons of Goliath, thought he could kill David. But Abishai the son of Zeruiah came to the King's rescue and killed the giant. David's men were very aware of his age and condition, for they said;

> *"You shall go out no more with us to battle,*
> *lest you quench the lamp of Israel."*
>
> 2 Samuel 21:17b

David headed the words of his fighting forces and returned to Jerusalem.

War continued against the Philistines, and the remaining three brothers of Goliath were also killed. King David was thankful for God intervening in his life and the lives of his people so David prayed to Father God for the restored favour He had afforded them.

> *"O God, You have cast us off;*
> *You have broken us down;*
> *You have been displeased;*
> *Oh, restore us again!*
> *You have made the earth tremble;*
> *You have broken it;*
> *Heal its breaches, for it is shaking.*
> *You have shown Your people hard things;*
> *You have made us drink the wine of confusion."*
>
> *"Give us help from trouble,*
> *for the help of man is useless.*
> *Through God we will do valiantly,*
> *for it is He who shall tread down our enemies."*
>
> Psalm 60:1-3, 11-12

During the final years of David's reign, he required a census of all the fighting men who were in his domain. It was

Satan and not God who prompted David's concern for his good reputation. Satan, not an angry God, incited David to sin. David was looking at numbers, rather than relying on Father God to supply everything he needed.

> *"Now Satan stood up against Israel,*
> *and moved David to number Israel.*
> *So David said to Joab and to the leaders of the people,*
> *'Go, number Israel from Beersheba to Dan,*
> *and bring the number of them to me that I may know it'."*
>
> 1 Chronicles 21:1-2

Because David had been deceived by Satan, God gave him three choices to repent for the sin he had committed. After much consideration, David chose *'for three days the sword of the Lord, the plague in the land, the angel of the Lord destroying throughout all the territory of Israel'.*

1 Chronicles 21:11

> *"So the Lord sent a plague upon Israel,*
> *and seventy thousand men of Israel fell.*
> *And God sent an angel to Jerusalem to destroy it.*
> *As he was destroying,*
> *the Lord looked and relented of the disaster,*

> *and said to the angel who was destroying,*
> *'It is enough; now restrain your hand'."*

1 Chronicles. 21:14

When David saw how his choice had impacted the people in his care, he spoke to the Lord when he saw the angel striking the people;

> *"Surely I have sinned, and I have done wickedly;*
> *but these sheep, what have they done?*
> *Let Your hand, I pray,*
> *be against me and against my father's house."*

2 Samuel 24:17b

David was required to carry out a sacrifice to the Lord God for the remission of his sin. The angel of the Lord commanded Gad, David's seer, to erect an altar to the Lord on the threshing floor of Ornan the Jebusite. When David approached Ornan, he was willing to give David everything he required without payment, but David refused the offer and paid for everything, including the place, wood and livestock. David sacrificed to the Lord as He was commanded, and after this was completed;

> *"The Lord commanded the angel,*
> *and he returned his sword to its sheath."*

1 Chronicles 21:27

King David was old and advanced in years. When he lay down, they put covers on him but he could not get warm so a young virgin, a Shunammite woman was brought to care for David. The young woman was lovely and cared for the king and served him, but the king did not know her.

Adonijah, the last remaining son from David's first marriage, assumed he would be the one to take the place of his father. He arranged sacrifices and a great banquet but omitted to invite those who counted the most. When Nathan the prophet found out what had taken place, he went to Bathsheba and reminded her of David's pledge to give the throne to Solomon on his death.

Bathsheba went to her husband, bowed and paid homage to him. David said, "What is your wish?" She outlined all that was about to happen and reminded David of his pledge. Nathan arrived and supported everything Bathsheba had told him so David proclaimed Solomon as his successor.

King David said, "Call to me Zadok the priest,
Nathan the prophet, and Benaiah the son of Jehoiada."
So they came before the king.
The king said, "Take with you the servants of the Lord,
and have Solomon my son ride on my mule,
and take him down to Gihon.

Betrayal

Let Zadok the priest and Nathan the prophet
anoint him king over Israel; and blow the horn,
and say, 'Long live King Solomon!'
Then you shall come up after him,
and he shall come and sit on my throne,
and he shall be king in my place.
For I have appointed him to be ruler over Israel and Judah."

1 Kings 1:32-35

When Adonijah was told Solomon's anointing had taken place while he and his guests were feasting and celebrating, he was afraid. All his guests were afraid and arose and each one went their way. Adonijah was afraid of Solomon and the ramifications for him and his family. Solomon sent word to Adonijah that if he proved himself a worthy man, he had nothing to fear.

Because Solomon was young and inexperienced, David called his son and outlined plans for the temple that he would build. The days of King David's rule of Israel finally came to an end, and he rested with his fathers and was buried in the City of David.

The period that David reigned over Israel was forty years; seven years in Hebron, and Jerusalem thirty-three years. Then Solomon sat on the throne of his father David, and his kingdom was firmly established.

Throughout the reign of King David, at least nine other prayers were uttered by him. It is uncertain when they were written, but with some diligence, suitable places could be found for their use and where they could be placed in David's life.

A Prayer for Guidance. Psalm 5

> *"Give ear to my words, O Lord,*
> *consider my meditation.*
> *Give heed to the voice of my cry,*
> *My King and my God,*
> *for to You I will pray."*

> *"But let all those rejoice who put their trust in You;*
> *Let them ever shout for joy,*
> *because You defend them;*
> *Let those also who love Your name*
> *be joyful in You.*
> *For You, O Lord, will bless the righteous;*
> *with favour You will surround him as with a shield."*
>
> Psalm 5:1-2, 11-12

Betrayal

A Prayer of Faith in Time of Distress. Psalm 6

> "O Lord, do not rebuke me in Your anger,
> nor chasten me in Your hot displeasure."

> "Return, O Lord, deliver me!
> Oh, save me for Your mercies' sake!"

> "Depart from me, all you workers of iniquity;
> For the Lord has heard the voice of my weeping.
> The Lord has heard my supplications;
> the Lord will receive my prayer.
> Let all my enemies be ashamed and greatly troubled;
> Let them turn back and be ashamed suddenly."
>
> Psalm 6:1, 4, 8-10

Prayer and Thanksgiving. Psalm 9

> "I will praise You, O Lord, with my whole heart;
> I will tell of all Your marvellous works.
> I will be glad and rejoice in You;
> I will sing praise to Your name, O most High."

David's Life of Prayer.

"Arise, O Lord,
do not let man prevail;
Let the nations be judged in Your sight.
Put them in fear, O Lord,
that the nations may know themselves to be but men."

Psalm 9:1-2, 19-20

Prayer with Confidence in Final Salvation. Psalm 17

"Hear a just cause, O Lord,
attend to my cry;
Give ear to my prayer
which is not from deceitful lips."

"You have tested my heart;
You visited me in the night;
You have tried me and have found nothing;
I have purposed that my mouth shall not transgress."

"I have called upon You,
for You will hear me, O God;
Incline Your ear to me,
and hear my speech.

Betrayal

Show Your marvellous lovingkindness
by Your right hand,
O You who save those who trust in You
from those who rise up against them."

"As for me, I will see Your face in righteousness;
I shall be satisfied when I awake in Your likeness."
Psalm 17:1, 3, 6-7, 15

Prayer for Divine Scrutiny and Redemption. Psalm 26

"Vindicate me, O Lord,
for I have walked in my integrity.
I have also trusted in the Lord;
I shall not slip.
Examine me, O Lord, and prove me;
try my mind and my heart."

"But as for me, I will walk in my integrity;
Redeem me and be merciful to me.
My foot stands in an even place;
in the congregations I will bless the Lord."
Psalm 26:1-2, 11-12

David's Life of Prayer.

Prayer in Time of Chastening. Psalm 38.

> "O Lord, do not rebuke me in Your wrath,
> nor chasten me in Your hot displeasure!"

> "Lord, all my desire is before You;
> and my sighing is not hidden from You.
> My heart pants, my strength fails me;
> as for the light of my eyes,
> it also has gone from me."

> "For in You, O Lord, I hope;
> You will hear, O Lord my God."

> "Do not forsake me, O Lord;
> O my God, be not far from me!
> make haste to help me,
> O Lord, my salvation."
>
> Psalm 38:1, 9-10, 15, 21-22

Prayer for Relief from Adversaries. Psalm 70

> "Make haste, O God, to deliver me!
> Make haste to help me, O Lord!

Let them be ashamed and confounded
who seek my life;
Let them be turned back and confused
who desire my hurt.
Let them be turned back because of their shame,
who say, "Aha, aha!"
Let all those who seek You rejoice and be glad in You;
and let those who love Your salvation say continually,
"Let God be magnified!"
But I am poor and needy;
make haste to me, O God!
You are my help and my deliverer;
O Lord, do not delay."

Psalm 70:1-5

Prayer for Mercy. Psalm 86

"Bow down Your ear, O Lord, hear me;
For I am poor and needy.
Preserve my life, for I am holy;
You are my God;
Save Your servant who trusts in You!
Be merciful to me, O Lord,
for I cry to You all day long."

David's Life of Prayer.

"Give ear, O Lord, to my prayer;
and attend to the voice of my supplications.
In the day of my trouble I will call upon You,
For Your will answer me."

"Teach me Your way, O Lord;
I will walk in Your truth;
Unite my heart to fear Your name."

"Show me a sign for good,
that those who hate me
may see it and be ashamed,
because You, Lord,
have helped me and comforted me."

Psalm 86:1-3, 6-7, 11, 17

Prayer for Safekeeping from Wickedness. Psalm 141

"Lord, I cry out to You; make haste to me!
Give ear to my voice when I cry out to You."

"Set a guard, O Lord, over my mouth;
Keep watch over the door of my lips."

> *"But my eyes are upon You, O God the Lord;*
> *in You I take refuge;*
> *Do not leave my soul destitute.*
> *Keep me from the snares they have laud for me,*
> *and from the traps of the workers of iniquity.*
> *Let the wicked fall into their own nets,*
> *while I escape safely."*
>
> Psalm 141:1, 3, 8-10

Conclusion.

From shepherd boy to King of Israel. The first book of Kings, although the author is unknown wrote the following about the life of David.

> *"David did what was right in the eyes of the Lord,*
> *and had not turned aside from anything*
> *that He commanded him all the days of his life,*
> *except in the matter of Uriah the Hittite."*
>
> 1 Kings 15:5

From the earliest time in his life, David was given responsibility for the sheep of his father, Jesse. David saw much when caring for the sheep as with his understanding of Father God. This was revealed when Samuel came to the home of Jesse to anoint the one who would take the place of King Saul.

David was the last to be called but, as the Lord has chosen him, Samuel anointed David with oil. We are told that;

> *"The Spirit of the Lord*
> *came upon David from that day forward."*
>
> 1 Samuel 16:13

One of the earliest psalms to be written was Psalm 23. The essence of the psalm provides the platform or foundation that established the life of David. He understood all his needs were met by Father God as God provided his protection. No matter where he found himself, Father God was his all-sufficiency. He knew that God would always be an ever-present help and companion through every struggle and temptation he was called to face.

As we progressed through each prayer, the psalm spoken by David, his life demonstrated his faith, trust and love for God. David remained faithful to the God who called him because his heart was pure. This didn't absolve him from temptation, and he faltered, as the verse said, once during his reign of Israel.

David was intimidated sometimes by others. When he arrived at the battle, Eliab ridiculed David. David wanted to understand and asked, "What have I done now?" Later, when

Saul wanted to kill David, he asked Jonathan why Saul wanted him dead. David said, "What have I done?"

David was very aware of the Holy Spirit's indwelling. When Nathan revealed to David the sin he had committed, as a man of God, David's real concern was that God would take the Holy Spirit away from him as he did to his predecessor, Saul.

David experienced the same things we do, such as grief and loss. However, David never questioned the path he was called to walk, but with each trial, his faith in God was strengthened.

David was not absolved from satanic attacks, as we read that Satan stood up against Israel and David faltered. Many paid the supreme price for David's decision, but in the end, David repented and was once again at peace with Father God. David cared for the sheep of his flock more than about himself.

Unlike Saul who never saw the necessity of repentance, David realized that the real relationship existed because one kept their heart clean and humbled oneself before Father God.

David's Prayer Psalms

Psalm	Chronological Order	Comment
23	1 Samuel 16:14-23	The distressing spirit troubles Saul.
56	1 Samuel 21:10-15	David's troublesome relationship with Saul. David fled to Gath.
57	1 Samuel 24:1-22	David's spared the life of Saul.
142	1 Samuel 24:1-22	David hiding in the cave.
54	1 Samuel 26:1 to 30:31	Answered prayer for deliverance from adversaries.
39	1 Chronicles 16:37-43	Prayer for Wisdom and Forgiveness.
51	2 Samuel 12:1-15	David reigned over both Judah and Israel. Nathan's Parable and David's confession.
3	2 Samuel 15:1-37	Prayer in time of trouble.
7	2 Samuel 16:1-14	Prayer and Praise for deliverance from Enemies.
60	1 Chronicles 18:14 to 20:8	Urgent Prayer for the restoration Favour of God.
5	1 Chronicles 21:1-30	Prayer for Guidance.
6	1 Chronicles 21:1-30	Prayer of Faith in time of distress.
9	1 Chronicles 21:1-30	Prayer and thanksgiving for the Lord's righteous Judgements.
17	1 Chronicles 21:1-30	Prayer with Confidence in Final Salvation.
26	1 Chronicles 21:1-30	Prayer for Divine Scrutiny and Redemption.
38	1 Chronicles 21:1-30	Prayer in time of Chastening.
70	1 Chronicles 21:1-30	Prayer for relief from Adversaries.
86	1 Chronicles 21:1-30	Prayer for Mercy, with Meditation on the excellencies of the Lord.
141	1 Chronicles 21:1-30	Prayer for safekeeping from wickedness.

David's Life of Prayer.

Similarities between David and Jesus known as the Son of David	
David	**Jesus**
Jewish tradition. David's birth not planned.	Born of the Holy Spirit through the virgin Mary.
David's family did not believe in him.	Jesus' family did not believe in Him.
David was anointed and filled with the Holy Spirit.	Jesus was baptised by John and filled with the Holy Spirit.
David enjoyed communion with the Holy Spirit.	Jesus was empowered with the power of the Holy Spirit.
Saul offered David his armour and sword.	Satan offered Jesus his kingdom. Bow down and worship me.
Johnathan gave David his armour and sword.	Jesus accepted His Father's way of the cross.
Saul tried to make David king in different ways.	Many tried to make Jesus reveal Himself before His time.
David knew what it was like to be popular.	Jesus knew what it was like to be popular.
David knew what it was like to be persecuted.	Jesus knew what it was like to be persecuted.
David was despised and rejected by many.	Jesus was despised and rejected by the majority.
David mostly sought the will of Father God.	Jesus always sought the will of the Father.
David walked over the Kidron Brook to the Mount of Olives.	Jesus walked over the Kidron Brook to the Mount of Olives.
David crossed the Jordon River.	Jesus crossed the Jordon River.
David prayed.	Jesus always prayed.
David had no fault found in him. 1 Samuel 29:3b	Jesus had no fault found in Him. Luke 23:4
David fought many physical battles.	Jesus fought many spiritual battles.
David received his earthly kingdom.	Jesus received His Spiritual kingdom.

Prayers in the Old Testament. Final Thoughts

As we have looked at the three sections, 'Prayers in the Old Testament', 'People Who Prayed', and 'David's Life of Prayer', the evidence has been presented, read and meditated upon. The question, "Who did all the people mentioned pray to?" and the second question, "Who answered the petitions made?" have now been answered.

It would appear that all three parts of the Godhead had significant parts to play, as they all acted as one on any God-ordained occasion. While Father God formulated His plan for mankind and their worship of Him, Jesus, as the *'Word'* spoke what His Father desired. The Holy Spirit supplied the *'Power'* to bring what the Father desired into existence.

On other occasions, various angels, named or unnamed were used to answer the prayers, and petitions prayed. While most people in the Old Testament did not understand the make-up of God, they accepted it was God whom they were speaking with and what He could accomplish was completed by Him. At other times, God sent messengers to convey His will.

One that has given me much food for thought is the angel that dispensed death. I refer to Egypt and the *'Passover'* and the last years of David's life, when the *'Angel of the Lord'* dispensed death to 70,000 men of Israel because of David's sin in succumbing to Satan's temptation.

When reading the account of the *'Passover'*, it appeared that Jesus, in His heavenly form, passed over all those in Egypt. When David was required to be punished for his second sin, the Lord gave the command which was obediently carried out. The difference between the two situations was that the Lord spoke to Moses and told him what precautions were to be observed, whereas on the occasion with David, it was judgment for sin committed.

Whether the angel was Jesus in His heavenly form or an angel God chose to use to carry out His will, is unsure, for we are not told.

Betrayal.

Betrayal is a painful and destructive experience that can cause deep wounds and long scars. Betrayal is a familiar theme in movies, in literature and in real life too. Betrayal usually involves individuals who were once trusted friends or even family members. People who were once close to the one who is betrayed. The Bible contains many stories about betrayal, lying, cheating, stealing and even murder. Betrayals that were motivated by jealousy, greed, lust, pride or a desire for power.

We will experience many trials and disappointments in life, but if we walk in God's ordained path we are assured that God has everything in His control. We may not see where the Holy Spirit is leading us, but in hindsight, all will become clear. A Bible verse that is helpful with our daily Christian walk is;

> *"A man's heart plans his way,*
> *but the Lord directs his steps."*
>
> Proverbs 16:9.

Jacob was not the firstborn and therefore by tradition would not inherit the birthright. The blessing given by a father to the firstborn determines their destiny in life so, what was Jacob to do? An opportunity presented itself when his elder brother Esau, who was a hunter of wild game, came home tired and empty-handed. He found Jacob at the tent cooking some delicious stew of lentils and because he was starving, the food was irresistible so, he asked for some and Jacob quickly took advantage.

Esau swore an oath to Jacob and sold his birthright for some stew. The Bible says, *"Esau despised his birthright"* (Genesis 25:30-34). Jacob later told his parents Esau had sold him his birthright but his father, Isaac disregarded it but, Rebekah, his mother took the agreement seriously, because God earlier informed her, even before the brothers were born, that the older would serve the younger. Genesis 25:23

Many years later when Isaac was old and wanted to pronounce his blessing on the firstborn, Rebekah advised Jacob to trick his nearly blind father to receive the blessing that was rightfully his. Jacob listened and after disguising himself in Esau's garments, served his father goat meat in place of his brother's game. Isaac had been deceived and Jacob received the blessing. Jacob was shrewdly planning his way but God was directing his steps elsewhere.

Betrayal.

When Esau returned, and found out about Jacob's trickery, he was filled with wrath and started plotting to kill Jacob. Long story short, Jacob had to flee from home and stay with a crafty uncle of his. God allowed him to experience the other side of trickery, so he could understand how much he had hurt his brother. For twenty years he served his uncle Laban but eventually, God delivered Jacob with great wealth and gave him a new name. He called him Israel. Genesis, chapters 27-32

Joseph shared the dreams he had with his brothers. He told them they would bow down before him, just like the sheaths of grain, and that the stars would do the same. Joseph didn't realise he was stirring up jealousy and envy in the hearts of his brothers. They hated Joseph and wished him dead.

The wishing turned into plotting, and the plotting turned into action. Eventually, the brothers grabbed Joseph and stripped him of his beautiful coat, threw him into a pit, and left him to die. Joseph was betrayed and sold by most of his brothers to the Ishmaelites as a slave.

As Joseph was saved from certain death, he eventually became ruler in Egypt. Some years later, Joseph was reunited with his brothers and family. The story of betrayal ended with forgiveness and a happy reunion. God's plan, His purpose had been worked out so that what seemed bad, ended up being good. Genesis, chapters 37-50

Joseph's life was a foreshadow of Jesus. We see this demonstrated in the following ways:

- Jesus was the object of His Father's love.
- He was mocked by His family.
- He was stripped of His robe.
- He was sold for thirty pieces of silver.
- He was delivered up to the Gentiles.
- He was falsely accused.
- He was faithful amid temptation.
- He stood before rulers.
- He embraced God's purpose even though it brought Him intense physical pain.
- He was the instrument Father God used at the hands of Gentiles to bless people.
- He welcomed Gentiles to be part of His family.
- He gave hungry people bread.
- People must bow their knees before Him.

So, we have looked briefly at Jacob and Joseph, with their respective God-ordained walks. But what about Judas? One of the last disciples to be called to follow Jesus after the night of prayer. Not much is known about this man until the end of Jesus' ministry. We are told that Judas was a Zealot, that he was in charge of the money and was a thief and a robber (John 12:6). Has it ever struck you as odd that Jesus put a thief in charge of His moneybag?

Betrayal.

Tension had mounted between the Jewish rulers and Jesus so, Judas arranged to deliver Jesus into their hands away from the crowds for thirty pieces of silver (Matthew 26:14-16, Mark 14:10-11). At the Last Supper, Jesus shared that one of His disciples would betray Him. Everyone in the room was capable of betrayal and denial. Matthew 26:22

Jesus had referred to the here and now, but Peter would also betray Him by denying his relationship with Jesus. All eleven disciples betrayed Jesus as they fled in the garden of Gethsemane.

After Peter had asked John to ask Jesus who would be the betrayer, Jesus answered, *"It is he to whom I shall give a piece of bread when I have dipped it."* And having dipped the bread, He gave it to Judas Iscariot, the son of Simon" (John 13:26-27). The question that needs to be asked is, 'Why didn't the disciples understand the answer Jesus gave?'

Only one understood what Jesus had said. If the other disciples had any idea to whom Jesus was referring, Judas would have never left the room. There is a verse Jesus had previously shared which said,

> *"Seeing they will not see,*
> *and hearing they will not hear or understand."*
>
> Luke 8:10

Another question could be, 'When did Judas sin?' Judas went to the authorities with good intentions to force Jesus' hand to overthrow the Romans. At any time, Judas could have foregone his plan, but it was only when Jesus said, *"What you do, do quickly"* (John 13:27b), Jesus gave permission for Judas to act and Satan was willing to do his best. Thoughts are not sins, but acting on a meditated thought is a sin.

Judas was the first to receive understanding, but not spiritual. Spiritual understanding came to the Centurion at the Cross (Matthew 27:54). John also received enlightenment at the tomb when he saw the napkin, folded in a place of its own (John 20:8). The two on the road to Emmaus were next, for we are told *"Then their eyes were opened"* (Luke 24:31). The ten disciples followed. John 20:19

Enlightenment continued to escalate until Pentecost when full understanding was given to all who accepted Jesus as their Lord and Saviour. The Holy Spirit would empower their life to live in victory as He does for us.

It is hard to imagine the Holy Spirit permits us to do something other than the revealed will of God. But then the thing we do may be in the will of God for our refining. We have free will to choose, even though we go on a downward path. After we have come to our senses and sought forgiveness, He aligns our path again with His. Always remember;

> *"A man's heart plans his way,*
> *but the Lord directs his steps."*
>
> Proverbs 16:9

Preparation Time.

The day or time set aside for preparation, whether it was for a Feast day or a Sabbath, was most important as all food was to be prepared in advance, so the Feast or Sabbath was given its rightful observance. Very strict rules had been implemented to ensure the day was observed with all due reverence.

The *'Preparation Time'* for the *'Passover'*, was carried out with meticulous preparations to ensure everything was ready for the true meaning of the feast to be celebrated. As we look at both the preparation and the *'Passover'* meal, we will discover some hidden truths. A suitable verse is;

> *"And He took bread, gave thanks and broke it,*
> *and gave it to them, saying,*
> *"This is My body which is given for you;*
> *do this in remembrance of Me'."*
> *Likewise He also took the cup after supper, saying,*
> *"This cup is the new covenant in My Blood,*
> *which is shed for you."*
>
> Luke 22:19-20

If you were a Jew, you would be celebrating the *'Passover'* in the evening at 6 pm until the following evening at 6 pm on the designated day set aside according to their calendar. We, on the other hand, celebrate Good Friday to Easter Monday with Sunday as the *'Resurrection'* of Jesus from the dead.

While some Christians choose to celebrate the *'Passover Feast'* followed by the *'Lord's Supper'* on the previous night, it is the *'Passover Day'* that holds so much that is often overlooked. When Jesus shared this night with His disciples, Luke leaves us in no doubt as while they were connected, they were two separate feasts. The *'Passover Feast'* (Luke 22:14-16), followed by the *'Lord's Supper'* (Luke 22:17-20).

To obtain a clear understanding of the events contained in the twenty-one hours, all four gospels need to be searched. This is what I found, beginning from Thursday, 6 pm to 3 pm the following day.

- The day of Preparation finished at 6 pm.
- Eating the Last Supper.
- Washing all the disciple's feet.
- Conversation with Judas about his betrayal.
- Institution of the Lord's Supper.
- Teaching and prayer time.
- Hymn sung.
- Walk to the Garden of Gethsemane.

Betrayal.

- Prayer time.
- Arrest and betrayal of Jesus.
- Examined by Annas.
- Jesus was tried by Caiaphas, the high priest and Sanhedrin.
- Taken to Pilate.
- Sent to Herod.
- Returned to Pilate and Judgment.
- Mockery by Roman soldiers.
- Led to Golgotha.
- Nailed to cross by 9 am.
- After six hours, Jesus committed Himself to His Father's care.

When you write it down, a lot happened in the very short time of twenty-one hours. As I meditate on these events, two questions come to mind. The first is, 'What psalm could have been used?' as this is mentioned twice (Matthew 26:30, Mark 14:26). The second question is, 'What is contained in the teaching Jesus shared at the Lord's Supper that could be of benefit to us all?' Let's look at the Psalms and see which ones would be the most likely.

A *'Passover'* meal included the singing of the Hallel, which was Psalms 113-118. According to the *'Passover'* tradition, those present sang Psalms 113-114 earlier in the meal and sang Psalms 115-118 after the meal. Soon Jesus would be praying in the garden of Gethsemane and then arrested, so the timing of these psalms is powerful when we consider their content.

Jesus could have sung Psalm 115:9-11.

> *"O Israel, trust in the Lord!*
> *He is their help and their shield.*
> *O house of Aaron, trust in the Lord!*
> *He is their help and their shield.*
> *You who fear the Lord, trust in the Lord!*
> *He is their help and their shield."*

Jesus could have sung Psalm 116:3-4.

> *"The pains of death surrounded me;*
> *the pangs of Sheol laid hold on me;*
> *I found trouble and sorrow.*
> *Then I called upon the name of the Lord:*
> *'O Lord, I implore You, deliver my soul!'"*

Jesus could have sung Psalm 118:5-7.

> *"I called on the Lord in distress;*
> *the Lord answered me in a broad place.*
> *The Lord is on my side; I will not fear.*

Betrayal.

What can man do to me?
The Lord is for me among those who help me;
Therefore, I shall see my desire on those who hate me."

Jesus could have sung Psalm 118:22.

"The stone which the builders rejected
has become the chief cornerstone.
This was the Lord's doing;
it is marvellous in our eyes."

The second question is 'What is the significance of Jesus leaving this teaching until now?' We need to look at John's Gospel to identify its significance. You can read this if you choose, John 14:1 to 16:33. Included with Jesus' teachings were His prayers for Himself, His disciples and all believers (John 17:1-26). As Jesus moved from *'The Passover'* to the *'Last Supper'*, He instigated a New Covenant. We need to ask, 'What was the old covenant it had replaced?'

The Old Testament was all about the Law and the keeping of it which was impossible for everyone except Jesus. Jesus was to institute a New Covenant which He brought about, as He obeyed the known will of His Father. The disciples had no idea about the importance of Jesus' new covenant, until Pentecost.

A New Covenant was the time when fresh revelation came to the disciples and those of the called. I guess you could say, this was moving from law to grace. Jesus said something about Himself not replacing the law.

"Do not think that I came to destroy the Law or the Prophets.
I did not come to destroy but to fulfil.
For assuredly, I say to you,
till heaven and earth pass away,
one jot or one tittle will by no means pass
from the law till all is fulfilled"

Matthew 5:17-18

Another word for 'fulfilled' is 'finished.' Do you remember Jesus' last words from the cross?

"After this, Jesus,
knowing that all things were now accomplished,
that the Scripture might be fulfilled,
said, 'I thirst!'
So when Jesus had received the sour wine,
He said, 'It is finished!'
And bowing His head,
He gave up His spirit."

John 19:28, v30

Betrayal.

It would be a good time to remember the words of Simeon so many years previously to Joseph and Mary.

> "Lord, my eyes have seen Your salvation
> which You have prepared before the face of all peoples,
> a light to bring revelation to the Gentiles,
> and the glory of Your people Israel."
>
> Luke 2:30-32

Jesus fulfilled Simeon's prophesy despite Satan's continual intervention in His life. As Satan was and is a defeated foe, the *Law* had been vanquished and *Grace* was ushered in.

The *'Day of Preparation'* is the day to prepare food for the *'Passover'*. The first must-attend feast for the Jews is *'The Feast of Unleavened Bread'*. It should be noted, that while the Jews observed and remembered the *'Passover'* and the significance for them, they were also commanded to observe the *'Feast of Unleavened Bread'* which is a nine-day feast time.

The feast began with *'Passover'*, followed by the *'Feast of Unleavened Bread'*, and the *'Feast of Firstfruits'* all on consecutive days. Unleavened bread must be eaten for the entire nine feast days.

There is a custom which is still observed in Jewish homes to this day. On the day of preparation, the home is maliciously cleaned and all leaven is removed completely. A couple of small pieces of leaven are hidden within the home. The father takes his children with only a candle to light the way to find the leaven pieces. When found, the children are forbidden to touch it. The father takes a feather and sweeps it onto the wooden spoon. This is all placed in a linen cloth and wrapped, taken outside and burned. Leaven in the Bible represents sin.

We are living in *'The Day of Preparation'*, and those of the called are being summoned to the *'Marriage Supper of the Lamb'*. When the Holy Spirit takes hold of us, He sheds the true Light on our heart to reveal those areas that need to be eradicated. Just as the feather was used to place the leaven on the wooden spoon, so our sins are taken and placed on the cross where Jesus died for our pardon and redemption. Just as Jesus was wrapped in linen, so too are our sins and shortcomings. Just as this wrapped package was then thrown into the fire and burned, so too are our sins thrown into the sea of God's forgetfulness. Micah 7:19

The Great High Priest.
The writer to the Hebrews assures us that Jesus Christ is the Great High Priest. By His suffering and death, along with His spotless life, was accepted by Father God as a suitable

sacrifice for the sin of mankind. We know this is true because, on the third day, Father God raised His Son from the dead. The writer to the Hebrews wrote;

> *"Seeing then that we have a great High priest*
> *who has passed through the heavens,*
> *Jesus the Son of God,*
> *let us hold fast our confession.*
> *For we do not have a High Priest*
> *who cannot sympathise with our weaknesses,*
> *but was in all points tempted as we are,*
> *yet without sin."*
>
> Hebrews 4:14-15

Jesus was taken before the Sanhedrin and Caiaphas, who was the high priest (Mark 14:53-65). One verse that stands out is *"Then the high priest tore his clothes."* This is recorded in verse 63a. The obvious question is, 'What significance does this have?' We need to search the Levitical law for an answer. *"He who is the high priest among his brethren, on whose head the anointing oil was poured and who is consecrated to wear the garments, shall not uncover his head nor <u>tear his clothes</u>."* Leviticus 21:10

By tearing his clothes, the high priest became ritually unclean. To regain his cleanliness, he must pass through a sunrise and a sunset. As Caiaphas was in a trial at about 2 am, this would be before sunrise. He would need to wait until the late afternoon, the twelfth hour or 6 pm to be ritually clean again.

There was no ritually clean high priest to conduct the further trials of Jesus. The father-in-law of Caiaphas was Annas, who was the retired high priest had conducted the first trial with Jesus. Annas was reinstated as high priest and continued to be for some time.

By sunset, Jesus had completed His earthly ministry. Jesus said, *"It is finished,"* bowed His head and died (John 19:30). This happened at the ninth hour or 3 pm. Three hours before sunset. There was no need for a high priest anymore, as Jesus has become our *Great High Priest*. Hebrews 4:14-16

The sacrificial system and all that was considered necessary by the religious people of the day, became obsolete once Jesus had died. He was the *'Sacrificial Lamb'* whose innocent blood paid, once and for all, the price God required for the sins of mankind.

Let's put this into context and order.
- The Jewish day began at sunset. Consider 6 pm as sunset for the discussion of events.

Betrayal.

- From 6 pm Wednesday night to 6 pm Thursday night was the day of *'Preparation for the Passover'*.
- From 6 pm Thursday night to 6 pm Friday night was the *'Passover'*.
- From 6 pm Friday night to 6 pm Saturday night was the Sabbath.
- A thing to note. That year, *'Passover'* and the *'Day of Preparation for the Sabbath'* were on the same day.
- 6 pm Saturday to 6 pm Sunday was not only the Sabbath but the second must-attend feast, *'The Feast of Unleavened Bread'*.
- 6 pm Sunday night to 6 pm Monday night was the third feast, *'The Feast of First Fruits'*.

Jesus sent Peter and John to prepare the Passover. 9 am to 6 pm on the Preparation day for the Passover which fell between Wednesday 6 pm to Thursday 6 pm.

Jesus met with His disciples for the *'Passover Feast'*, which would take place between 6 pm Thursday to 6 pm Friday. But much more transpired between these hours.

The *'Passover'* meal and teaching would be finished at about 10:00 pm. After singing a song, the eleven disciples left the Passover room, walked to the Garden of Gethsemane over the Kidron Brook, and arrived around 11:30 pm. Jesus left His disciples to pray, then continued on a little further to pray.

From the Upper Room in Jerusalem, which is 785 meters above sea level, the road descends to the Kidron Valley and crosses the Kidron Brook which is 450 meters below sea level. You then travel up to the Garden of Gethsemane which is approximately 700 meters above sea level.

Around 1 pm, Jesus is arrested and taken to Annas for the first of six trials He would endure, then to Caiaphas the high priest. These trials would be over by around 8 am. By 9 am, Jesus had walked to Golgotha and was nailed to the Cross for crucifixion. At noon, darkness came. At 3 pm or the ninth hour, Jesus entrusts His Spirit to the Father and dies.

Once Jesus had died, the veil in the temple ripped from top to bottom. Jesus, as the perfect sacrifice, had paid the price required by His Father. As the veil was in two pieces, direct access into the *'Holy of Holies'* was open. No longer would an earthly priest be required to enter this area on *'Yon Kippa'*. Caiaphas had removed himself and Annas had no right to assume this role. Jesus took the place of the earthly high priest and became our Great High Priest. There were three hours of the Passover day left before Caiaphas would be ritually clean.

Jesus now went and preached to those in Hades and took them to Paradise (1 Peter 3:19). Because Jesus is the *'Sacrificial Lamb'*, He had taken back the keys from Death and Hades. Revelation 1:17-18

The second must-attend feast, *'The Feast of Unleavened Bread'* would now take place. Leaven represents sin, therefore no bread with leaven is consumed. Jesus had paid the debt with His blood, which made the way open for all to have forgiveness through His shed blood. The leaven is now removed from the curse of the law.

Because Jesus was triumphant by the life He lived and the Perfect sacrifice given, *'The Feast of Fruit Fruits'* took place and Jesus was resurrected from the grave.

Jesus said, *"Three days and three nights in the grave as Jonah"* (Matthew 12:40). Does this work?

The *'Passover'* was the first day. Jesus died at 3 pm and this represented the last three hours of the first day.

'The *'Feast of Unleavened Bread'* was the second day.

The *'Feast of First Fruits'* was the third day. Mary had gone very early to the tomb on the day that followed the Sabbath which was the third day (John 20:1). 6 pm the previous night to maybe 3 am the next morning represented the third day. Jesus never said anything about three full days. Three partial days work well.

The *Passover* is all about Jesus and Him being the perfect sacrifice. The *Feast of Unleavened Bread* is about us now able to obtain forgiveness for our sins. Sin and leaven have been eradicated for those who believe. The *Feast of First Fruits* is all about Jesus, as He was the First Fruit.

Because all this transpired, Jesus, the unblemished Lamb, the Son of God, paid the price of our sins. Because the veil in the temple was rent from top to bottom, Jesus made the way open for us to have direct access into the very throne room of Father God. Jesus has once and for all become *"Our Great High Priest"*. Hallelujah!

Six Trials of Jesus.

Between the arrest of Jesus in the Garden of Gethsemane and 9 am when He was nailed to the cross, Jesus had 'Six Trials' to contend with.

When the armed mob arrived to arrest Jesus, although there was some opposition from a couple of disciples, Jesus peacefully surrendered into the hands of those who sought Him. Jesus was bound and then led to the residence of Annas the former high priest. One would imagine, that Annas had assumed the office of High Priest because his son-in-law was too afraid. This could have been in the vicinity of 2 am. By about 2:30 am, Jesus was in the home of the son-in-law, Caiaphas. After Jesus confessed to being the Messiah, Caiaphas became so enraged he tore his clothes.

Betrayal.

Days and Events in the Easter Season.

6pm Wednesday to 6pm Thursday.	6pm Thursday to 6pm Friday.	6pm Friday to 6pm Saturday.	6pm Saturday to 6pm Sunday.
Day of Preparation for the Passover.	Passover Eaten. Jesus arrested in garden. Six trials between 1 am and 8 am. Nailed to cross at 9 am. Died at 3 pm. Jesus buried in tomb.		Early Sunday morning Mary found the empty tomb. Jesus appeared to Mary outside the tomb. Jesus appeared to the two at Emmaus. Jesus appeared to the eleven disciples.
	Day of Preparation for the Sabbath.	Sabbath.	
	Feast of Passover.	Feast of Unleavened Bread.	Feast of First Fruits.

273

The third trial was before the Sanhedrin. They were seventy men who formed the Supreme Court of the Jews. To assemble so many would have taken some time. We are told this took place when it was day, which was possibly about 4:30 am. At around 6 am, the fourth trial took place for we read *'when the morning had come.'* This was where Jesus was interrogated by Pilate, the leading Roman official.

When Pilate established that Jesus was a Galilean, he sent Him to Herod Antipas, the governor of Galilee who just happened to be in Jerusalem, for Jesus' fifth trial which could have been about 6:30 am. Herod was pleased to see Jesus because of what he had heard. He thought Jesus might perform some miracle for him, but when Jesus said and did nothing, Herod and his men treated Jesus with contempt, and sent Him back to Pilate. This is now the sixth trial for Jesus and around 7 am.

Although Pilate could find no fault with Jesus, the fact that Jesus had admitted to being a King, meant in the eyes of Pilate, Jesus had committed treason against Rome. Wiping his hands of this predicament, Pilate handed Jesus over to his soldiers to make sport and to scourge Him. Once this was completed, they were to take Jesus to Golgotha and there, crucify Him. The time would be 9 am.

This is a brief account of the events. Let us once again move through each part to discover much that was not evident in the first reading.

The Garden of Gethsemane.

Jesus was well aware of what was about to take place. With His disciples, He moved forward to the mob and confronted them. *Jesus said to them, "Whom are you seeking?" They answered Him, "Jesus of Nazareth." Jesus said to them, "I am He." When He said to them, "I am He," they drew back and fell to the ground. Then He asked them again, "Whom are you seeking?" And they said, "Jesus of Nazareth." Jesus answered, "I have told you that I am He. Therefore, if you seek Me, let these go their way."* John 18:4-8

"Then the detachment of troops and the captain and the officers of the Jews arrested Jesus and bound Him. And they led Him away to Annas first, for he was the father-in-law of Caiaphas who was high priest that year." John 18:12-13

First Trial. Examined by Annas.

Annas was the retired high priest and had been for some time. He was also the father-in-law to Caiaphas the present high priest. It would appear that Annas was the instigator of Jesus' arrest, as he was not surprised when the soldiers, accompanied by the mob, arrived with Jesus and barged into his home sometime after midnight.

Annas was the first to examine Jesus and asked Him about His disciples and His doctrine. Jesus answered;

> *"I spoke openly to the world.*
> *I always taught in synagogues and in the temple,*
> *where the Jews always meet,*
> *and in secret I have said nothing.*
> *Why do you ask Me?*
> *Ask those who have heard Me what I said to them.*
> *Indeed they know what I said."*
>
> John 18:20-21

When Jesus answered truthfully, one of the officers struck Jesus with the palm of his hand. This was the first abuse that Jesus would suffer. Annas then sent Jesus bound to his son-in-law, Caiaphas the reigning high priest for further interrogation.

Second Trial. Trial by Caiaphas.

As it has already been established, Caiaphas was the son-in-law of Annas. In all likelihood, Annas mentored his son-in-law, instructing him in all things religious. Annas could have led the mob to the house of Caiaphas. Again, Caiaphas was not concerned about the time of night when they came knocking.

It should be noted that the scribes and the elders were already assembled with Caiaphas (Matthew 26:57). Caiaphas continued the interrogation where Annas finished. He appeared to be more hot-headed than Annas, unable to control his temper. Maybe this was due to a lack of sleep or spurred on by his father-in-law.

Caiaphas produced false witnesses to accuse Jesus and Jesus was asked many questions, but He answered nothing. In desperation, Caiaphas asked Jesus directly, *"Are You the Christ, the Son of the Blessed?"* To which Jesus replied,

"I am.

And you will see the Son of Man sitting
at the right hand of the Power,
and coming with the clouds of heaven."

Matthew 27:64

When Caiaphas heard the reply of Jesus he became so enraged that he tore his clothes, saying, *"He has spoken blasphemy! What further need do we have of witnesses? Look, now you have heard His blasphemy!"* (Matthew 26:65). After this, Jesus was subjected to more violence, but then Caiaphas tore his clothes and was no longer fit to be the high priest. By tearing his clothes, he defiled himself. In his anger, he broke the Levitical law which they so eagerly professed.

Levitical law says, *"He who is the high priest among his brethren, on whose head the anointing oil was poured and who is consecrated to wear the garments, shall not uncover his head nor <u>tear his clothes</u>."* Leviticus 21:10

Caiaphas had severed himself by the act of rage for the period of sunrise to sunset. The time was in the early morning and the daybreak was about to happen. He would be unclean until late afternoon at sundown or around 6 pm.

But someone else was needed to lead these proceedings against Jesus. They had His confession, but what were they to do? Annas was reinstated to carry out the priestly duties of his son-in-law, as he was the only one still alive who had been anointed. But unfortunately, while this was carried out, the law was again broken.

The law says, *"From twenty-five years old and above one may enter to perform service in the work of the tabernacle of meeting; and at the age of fifty years they must cease performing this work, and shall work no more. They may minister with their brethren in the tabernacle of meeting, to attend to needs, but they themselves <u>shall do no work</u>."* Numbers 8:24-26a

'Do as I say, not as I do' was the attitude portrayed as everyone agreed as Annas took the reins from his son-in-law and continued to do so for some time. The type of priest Annas displayed is one who would have held on to his office to the last possible moment. This meant he would be well and truly over fifty. He used his influence to take leadership although he broke the law prescribed for priests. As nothing more could be done, Caiaphas sent Jesus to the Sanhedrin for further examination and the third trial.

Third Trial. Condemnation by the Sanhedrin.

The previous two trials were illegal because they were held in the night hours, so the Sanhedrin conveniently convened a daylight trial, even though it was early. According to the Pentateuch and the Mishnah, the way they did this contravened the law. No trial was to be held on the day of the preparation for the Sabbath or a feast day. Sacrifices were also carried out before doing anything. This year, the *'Passover'* and the *'Preparation for the Sabbath'* were on the same day. This just gets better and better.

The third trial was to legitimise the coerced findings of the previous two. The Sanhedrin found Jesus guilty of blasphemy without observing the laws written for them to observe. These are the people who searched the law and turned it into hundreds of additional or minor laws to substantiate their teaching. They knew all the loopholes and used them to their advantage.

Because the Jews were under Roman rule, the Sanhedrin had no power to carry out executions. This was controlled by the Romans. Because the religious leaders wanted Jesus dead, they sought the death penalty at the hands of the Romans. So, they took Jesus, with their false claim of blasphemy to Pilate for his sanction.

Fourth Trial. Appearance before Pilate.

Pilate was the Roman governor of the district which included Jerusalem. He was ruthless with punishments, unbending, and had a notorious reputation for brutality. Rome was investigating Pilate for his handling of punishment, which meant Pilate was treading carefully.

The Sanhedrin or mob rule;

> "Began to accuse Him, saying,
> 'We found this fellow perverting the nation,
> and forbidding to pay taxes to Caesar,
> saying the He Himself is Christ, a King'."
>
> Luke 23:2

Pilate was not interested in the trumped-up charge of blasphemy, as the Romans worshipped many gods. When those who accused Jesus mentioned the word 'King', the whole situation changed as this was treason against Rome and Caesar. When Pilate asked Jesus directly if He was a King, Jesus answered, *"It is as you say"* (v3). Even with this confession, Pilate said to the chief priests and the crowd, *"I find no fault in this Man."* (v4)

> *But they were the more fierce, saying,*
> *"He stirs up the people,*
> *teaching throughout all Judea,*
> *beginning from Galilee to this place."*
>
> Luke 23:5

It was only when the accusers mentioned Jesus was a Galilean, that the situation changed. Jesus as a Galilean came under Herod's jurisdiction. This would relieve Pilate of any dealing with Jesus and remove any responsibility from him and the crimes they said He had committed, especially now it involved treason. So, Pilate sent the delegation to Herod, who just happened to be in Jerusalem, for his verdict.

Fifth Trial. Jesus appears before Herod.

We need to remember some things about this man Jesus is about to stand before. Herod respected Jesus' second cousin

John the Baptist even though John had exposed the wrong Herod had done. It was because of Herod's wife Herodias, that John was imprisoned, then later beheaded.

We are told Herod was glad to see Jesus as he had heard much about Him. Herod hoped He would do some miracle, but after asking many questions, he received no answers. Herod along with his men of war mocked Jesus, arrayed Him in a gorgeous robe, and sent Him back to Pilate for further judgment.

We have no idea why Herod was in Jerusalem, but it is recorded that Pilate and Herod became friends that day, whereas before there was tension between them both (Luke 23:12). Pilate showed courtesy and respect to Herod with one of his subjects, and mended the rift between them. Possibly Pilate had mistreated other subjects of Herod's with no mercy, and this was the reason behind the visit. Herod did have his men of war with him. This wasn't a social visit.

Sixth Trial. Jesus' second appearance before Pilate.

Pilate was not prepared for what was about to confront him. When Jesus returned, Pilate remembered a custom that the Jews had of releasing a condemned person. Pilate said, *"Do you want me to release to you the King of the Jews?" Then they cried out, "Not this man, but Barabbas!"* John 18:39-40

Pilate was of all men concerned about the innocence of Jesus. While he was ruthless with many who had previously stood before him, Jesus was different, besides, Pilate knew the religious leaders were acting out of hatred and jealousy. To further add to Pilate's confusion, *"While he was sitting on the judgement seat, his wife sent to him, saying, 'Have nothing to do with that just Man, for I have suffered many things today in a dream because of Him'."* Matthew 27:19

Pilate's soldiers scourged Jesus, secured a crown of thorns to His head and placed the purple robe on Him. Pilate said, *"Behold, I am bringing Him out to you, that you may know that I find no fault in Him"* (John 19:4). Pilate presented Jesus to them all and said, *"Behold the Man!"* (v5) While the crowd cried out to crucify Jesus, it was when Pilate heard them say, *"He made Himself the Son of God,"* this man of war became more afraid. John 19:7b-8

Pilate questioned Jesus again asking Him where was He from. After Jesus answered, Pilate wanted to release Jesus. But this all changed in the twinkling of an eye. So, what did Pilate hear that he dreaded the most?

"If you let this Man go, you are not Caesar's friend. Whoever makes himself a king speaks against Caesar." (v12a) What a dilemma for Pilate. He was already under investigation from Rome. This could end his career. So, Pilate washed his hands

of the whole ordeal and gave Jesus over to the Jewish rulers to be crucified.

More about the falseness of the trial.

There are many other details to consider. Bribery, illegal timing, and abuse are just three of a number. But let us take a closer look at Caiaphas first and then Annas.

When Jesus answered Caiaphas, *"I am. And you will see the Son of Man sitting at the right hand of the Power, and coming with the clouds of heaven,"* He was referring to a time in the future when Caiaphas would kneel before Him at the judgement. Not only was Jesus claiming to be with God, it would be He, who would be judging Caiaphas. How often has the first part of Jesus' reply, *"I am"*, been focused on, and the second part overlooked?

Caiaphas with his inflated ego, could not conceal his inward emotion and in rage, tore his clothes. This was ordained by Father God to remove the high priest from office, as Jesus would, in a very short time, become the Great High Priest for eternity.

Annas appeared to be the motivational force behind his son-in-law. He also had an over-inflated ego of his importance. At fifty years of age, he should have relinquished his

Betrayal.

office and become a support, but he became the driving force. He remained in the background and manipulated Caiaphas to do his bidding.

Annas was the first to question Jesus, not Caiaphas. When his son-in-law tore his priestly robes, this was exactly what Annas wanted and seized the opportunity to once again take leadership as the high priest, as there was no other alive who had been anointed. It would have been easy to convince the other members of the Sanhedrin, as they needed a high priest and, reinstating Annas was a quick solution.

It would appear that while Caiaphas would be ritually clean again after sundown that afternoon, he was not immediately reinstated to the high priest. *'Pentecost'* or the *'Feast of Weeks'* had passed and some more weeks besides. We read in the book of Acts the following.

> *"And it came to pass, on the next day,*
> *that their rulers, elders, and scribes,*
> *as well as Annas the high priest,*
> *Caiaphas, John, and Alexander,*
> *and as many were the family of the high priest,*
> *were gathered together at Jerusalem."*
>
> Acts 4:5-6

Annas was still heavily involved with the political-religious system he had spearheaded. He had instigated the death of Jesus, but by doing so, had inadvertently unleashed a *'Power'* well out of his control. He could do no more than bow to the finding of the Sanhedrin, the Jewish ruling council. What a different council to the one accusing Jesus of blasphemy. No spitting or punching. No brutality in any form, just harsh words. You would remember that many of this group believed in Jesus (John 12:42-43). I wonder how many were changed at Pentecost?

The legality of Jesus' trials is somewhat in doubt.

While much has been shown that would expose the absurdity of those who were the religious leaders with not only understanding the law, teaching the law, but living a life they thought was acceptable, there are still other areas to be searched for truth. Either what's to be found will further condemn these so-called religious leaders or will exonerate them.

It was Caiaphas who told the Sanhedrin council previously;

"You know nothing at all,
nor do you consider that it is expedient for us

that one man should die for the people,
and not that the whole nation should perish.
Then, from that day on, they plotted to put Him to death"

John 11:49b-50, 53

While they were plotting the death of Jesus, those involved had to be seen as keeping the law, after all, they were the religious leaders and the teachers of the law. They knew that Jesus could not be arrested and brought to trial if bribery was involved. Moses had written, *"You shall take no bribe, for a bribe blinds the discerning and perverts the words of the righteous"* (Exodus 23:8). Those in authority such as Judges or the ruling council were subject to the following. *"You shall not pervert justice; you shall not show partiality, nor take a bribe, for a bribe blinds the eyes of the wise and twists the words of the righteous."* Deuteronomy 16:19

These laws were conveniently overlooked when Judas showed up. *"Then one of the twelve, called Judas Iscariot, went to the chief priests and said, 'What are you willing to give me if I deliver Him to you?' And they counted out to him thirty pieces of silver. So from that time he sought opportunity to betray Him"* (Matthew 26:14-16). As they accepted Judas's offer and payment of thirty pieces of silver to betray Jesus, this constituted a bribe and delegitimized Jesus's trial.

Timing of the first three trials.

There were certain protocols which had to be observed. The observance of the feasts was a must. As they arrested Jesus on *'Passover'*, this was the first day of the nine-day feast of *'Unleavened Bread'*, which meant they could do nothing till after the nine days had passed. The risk was too high to wait this length of time, as word would have spread and many would have gathered and exposed their conspiracy to kill the Man many thought to be the Messiah.

The Pharisees or the Sanhedrin never thought that the long-awaited Messiah could be Jesus. They knew that their conspiracy with Judas to kill Jesus would quickly be general knowledge. These men had too much to lose so law after law was flaunted.

The Mishnah is the first major collection of Jewish oral traditions. It held as much authority as did the Mosaic Law. The writings clearly state that all trials were to be held in the daytime. This meant that the first two trials were illegitimate and the third was convened to suit the law, being held in the early daylight.

Another law of Moses said;

> *"Now this is what you shall offer on the altar:*
> *two lambs of the first year, day by day continually.*
> *One lamb you shall offer in the morning,*
> *and the other lamb you shall offer at twilight."*
>
> Exodus 29:38-39

The twice-daily offerings served to signify each day was to be opened and closed with gifts of worship to God. Nothing was to be done before this offering was made. Because the third trial was conducted before the morning sacrifice had been carried out, it would also be deemed illegal. Any decision made would be inadmissible in a real court of law.

Let us remember the words of Jesus when He said,

> *"And this is the condemnation,*
> *that the light has come into the world,*
> *and men loved darkness rather than light,*
> *because their deeds were evil."*
>
> John 3:19

Abuse of Jesus and how he was treated by His own.

Father God had foreseen evil in the hearts of men and put many laws in place to guard against much that men would be tempted to do and commit. By adhering to God's standards, His chosen people would or should be secure from each other. Let me share some verses of scripture relating to the abuse of a prisoner.

"You shall not steal, nor deal falsely, nor lie to one another" Leviticus 19:11

"You shall not cheat your neighbour, nor rob him." Leviticus 19:13a

"You shall not curse the deaf, nor put a stumbling block before the blind, but shall fear your God: I am the Lord." Leviticus 19:14

"You shall not hate your brother in your heart." Deuteronomy 19:17a

"You shall not take vengeance,
nor bear any grudge against the children of your people,
but you shall love your neighbour as yourself:
I am the Lord." Deuteronomy 19:18a

"You shall do no injustice in judgment." Deuteronomy 19:35a

So, let's put this together as it applies to Judges (Exodus 18:21) and priests. Leviticus 10:3, 22:9

- Not dealing falsely with other people. Leviticus 19:11
- Not oppressing your neighbour. Leviticus 19:13
- Not hurting the weak. Leviticus 19:14
- Not hating your fellow countryman in your heart. Leviticus 19:17
- Not taking vengeance upon the sons of your people. Leviticus 19:18a
- Not holding a grudge against the sons of your people. Leviticus 19:18b
- Not being unfair. Leviticus 19:35-36

In a previous conversation Jesus had with a scribe, he asked Jesus about the greatest commandment. Jesus asked him what he understood and the lawyer replied,

> *"You shall love the Lord your God with all your heart,*
> *with all your soul, with all your strength,*
> *and with all your mind,*
> *and your neighbour as yourself."*
>
> Luke 10:27

The scribe agreed with Jesus about the greatest commandment (Luke 10:25-28). To *"Love your neighbour as you love yourself"* (Leviticus 19:18b). If this was understood by the Pharisees and the scribes, who formed the Sanhedrin, when dealing with people, there is only one word that can be used to describe them, and that is 'Hypocrite'. Jesus warned

His disciples about the Pharisees and their hypocrisy when He said,

> *"Beware of the leaven of the Pharisees,*
> *which is hypocrisy.*
> *For there is nothing covered*
> *that will not be revealed,*
> *nor hidden that will not be known."*
>
> Luke 12:1b-2

Jesus was aware of the inward condition of the Pharisees and the scribes because when Jesus spoke to the disciples and the multitudes, within twenty-one verses He referred to them as hypocrites, seven times. Matthew 23:13-33

The first recorded abuse of Jesus was when He was struck for asking Annas to produce his witnesses against Him as was lawfully required for a proper trial. We read, *"When Jesus had said these things, one of the officers who stood by struck Jesus with the palm of his hand, saying, 'Do You answer the high priest like that?' Jesus answered him, 'If I have spoken evil, bear witness of the evil; but if well, why do you strike Me?'"* John 18:22-23

A second recorded abuse came at the end of the false night trial in the house of Caiaphas while Jesus was held, as he waited for the daylight trial of the Sanhedrin. There are two accounts. *"Then they spat in His face and beat Him; and others struck Him with the palms of their hands, saying, 'Prophesy to us, Christ! Who is the one who struck You?'"* (Matthew 26:67-68). *"Then some began to spit on Him, and to blindfold Him, and to beat Him, and to say to Him, 'Prophesy!' And the officers struck Him with the palms of their hands"* (Mark 14:65). Spitting, beating or punching, striking with their hands, all spoke of mob rule, as everyone was spurred on by the other.

While abuse was carried out, Jesus did not retaliate. He knew it was God's will for Him to suffer at the hands of evil men (Matthew 20:18-20). Jesus practised what He taught as He turned the other cheek (Matthew 5:39). Isaiah prophesied that the Messiah would suffer in silence.

> *"He was oppressed and He was afflicted,*
> *yet He opened not His mouth"*
>
> Isaiah 53:7a

Isaiah further prophesied about Jesus when he wrote;

> *"The Lord God has opened My ear;*
> *and I will not be rebellious,*
> *nor did I turn away.*
> *I gave My back to those who struck Me,*

> *and My cheeks to those who plucked out My beard;*
> *I did not hide My face from shame and spitting."*
>
> Isaiah 50:5-6

The abuse of Jesus had nothing to do with justice but was done in anger for their entertainment. Their act of hatred was a direct violation of the law, as to how people were to be treated (Leviticus 19:11-18). Whether Jesus was justly condemned or innocent, the actions of those who were in charge of Him were inexcusable and unjustifiable.

Solomon wrote wise words that spotlight this whole situation.

> *"Six things the Lord hates, yes,*
> *seven are an abomination to Him:*
> *A proud look, a lying tongue,*
> *hands that shed innocent blood,*
> *a heart that devises wicked plans,*
> *feet that are swift in running to evil,*
> *a false witness who speaks lies,*
> *and one who sows discord among brethren."*
>
> Proverbs 6:16-19

You may find it profitable to read the preceding verses, Proverbs 6:12-15.

While Solomon wrote about six things the Lord hates, those who were the instigators and the other leaders involved, were also guilty of the seven deadly sins. Pride. Lust. Greed. Envy. Sloth or laziness. Wrath or anger. Gluttony. Most of these seven deadly sins are self-explanatory, but to redefine Sloth, they were lazy in not searching out the real meaning of the law. Gluttony was just not about food, but also about their rights which they saw as privileges. When you look at their motivation, all seven can clearly be seen.

Conclusion.

Betrayal has always been a part of world history. In the heavenly places, Satan and his angels betrayed God. Eve betrayed her husband. Cain betrayed Abel. Job's friends betrayed him in his time of need. I have mentioned Jacob and Joseph. Daniel was betrayed because of jealousy and pride. Moses by his sister Miriam, who thought she should be above or equal with her little brother. David betrayed Uriah. Slept with Bathsheba and then had Uriah killed. Zachariah was betrayed and stoned.

Peter betrayed Jesus in the courtyard, and so did all the disciples in the garden. Saul (Paul) watched as Stephen was betrayed and then stoned. Are we then disturbed that the same would happen to our Lord? Paul when writing to the

Romans said, *"We are killed all day long."* Much betrayal was happening to the early Christians.

Traitors betray their country. Some spies work for both sides. How many Jews were betrayed and massacred in the Second World War? It would appear that the Jewish nation has suffered persecution forever.

Are we aware and expect that a time in the future will come when we will be betrayed for our faith? Prophecy is written to forewarn us about this time of testing. People will go to all lengths to secure their agenda at our cost. Only the faithful, a remnant, the called will survive, but not in this life.

With betrayal seen as normal practice in our modern society, husbands and wives prove unfaithful because they can. Those who are entitled betray those who don't agree with their perspective on life. Some parents betray the child in the womb, because of selfishness. Justice and the law are perverted to suit the minority to the detriment of those who love and serve Jesus Christ.

Always take heart in the fact that *"A man's heart plans his way, but the Lord directs his steps."* God is always in control no matter how bleak the situation may seem. We should always remember that;

Betrayal.

> *"All things work together for good*
> *to those who love God,*
> *to those who are the called*
> *according to His purpose."*
>
> Romans 8:28

Trials and Outcome of Jesus

Sequence	Investigation and Penalty	Outcome	Notes	Time
Arrested in the Garden of Gethsemane.	Sought Jesus.	Arrested. Led away bound to Annas.		1 am
1. Trial by Annas.	Examined.	Sent to son-in-law Caiaphas.	Annas was the previous high priest.	2 am
2. Trial by Caiaphas.	Questioned and Interrogated.	Caiaphas enraged. Tore his clothes. Sent Jesus to Sanhedrin.	By tearing his clothes, Caiaphas became ritually unclean and therefore ceased from any further involvement with Jesus. Annas took the place of Caiaphas. Leviticus 21:10 is the law governing this act.	2:30 am
3. Trial by Sanhedrin.	Blasphemy.	Found guilty.	This trial held in daylight was illegal.	4:30 am
4. Trial by Pilate.	Questioned.	Pilate recognised that Jesus is a Galilean and therefore sent Him to Herod who is in charge of Galilee.		6 am

Betrayal.

5. Trial by Herod.	Questioned.	Made sport of Jesus. Put on Him a purple robe. Sent Jesus back to Herod.	6:30 am
6. Trial by Pilate.	Questioned and Interrogated.	Found Innocent. Because Pilate feared offending Caesar, he gave Jesus over to the Jews to crucify.	Pilate was aware the Jewish leaders were jealous of Jesus and His ministry. Because Jesus had answered Pilate that He was a King, this was treason against Caesar and Rome.	7:00 am
Given to Soldiers.	They made sport of Jesus and scourged Him.	Bleeding, bruised. A crown of thorns on His head.	Jesus was redressed. The purple seamless robe given to Him by Herod adorned Him.	8:00 am
Taken to be crucified.	Nailed on the Cross at 9 am	Jesus died after committing His spirit to Father God. The veil in the temple torn in two.	There was no high priest. When Jesus died, the veil ripped from top to bottom. Jesus paid the price. He is now our Great High Priest.	3 pm

Note. The times are approximate only.

Judas the Betrayer.

As you read the different accounts in the four Gospels and the first chapter of Acts, about Judas betraying Jesus, there may appear to be some areas of conflict. One of these is when and how Judas died. While most accept that when Judas saw Jesus condemned, he went out and hung himself, other facts need to be considered and placed in a timeline.

The first thing to consider is the timing of Judas' visit to the High Priest and the governing body or the Sanhedrin. The disciple Matthew when writing his gospel, wrote the following information.

"Then one of the twelve, called Judas Iscariot, went to the chief priests and said, 'What are you willing to give me if I deliver Him to you?' And they counted out to him thirty pieces of silver. So from that time he sought opportunity to betray Him." Matthew 26:14-16

Judas bided his time always looking for that opportune moment when Jesus would be alone from the crowds and vulnerable. Judas thought, as did most of those of his era, that the Messiah would be a 'Warrior King' who would defeat the Romans and bring freedom and a physical release from oppression to the Jews as a nation. However, Father God instigated a spiritual release for mankind, but Judas thought by delivering Jesus into the hands of the religious leaders, he would force Jesus to reveal His identity as the Messiah.

Perhaps Judas thought the *'Passover Feast'* would be the best time for Jesus to be arrested, as they would be alone and in front of His disciples would show His pre-eminence. But this did not happen, as Jesus had prearranged a secret place for them all to be.

Jesus chose Peter and John to find a man carrying a waterpot who would lead them to the place Jesus had chosen for their supper together (Luke 22:10). Only when Jesus led His ten disciples to the prepared room was Judas aware of the location.

As the Passover meal progressed, Jesus said, *"Most assuredly, I say to you, one of you will betray Me"* (John 13:21). *"John then said to Jesus, 'Lord, who is it?' Jesus answered, 'It is he to whom I shall give a piece of bread when I have dipped it'. And having dipped the bread, He gave it to Judas Iscariot, the son of Simon"* (John 13:25b-26). *"Then Judas, who was betraying Him, answered and said, 'Rabbi, is it I?'"* (Matthew 26:25). *"Jesus said to him, 'You have said it'. Now after Judas accepted the piece of bread, Satan entered him. Then Jesus said to him, 'What you do, do quickly'."* John 13:27

When the *'Passover'* and the *'Lord's Supper'* were over, Jesus and His eleven disciples left and walked to the Garden of Gethsemane. When Judas returned to where the *'Passover'* was held, nobody was there as they had vacated the room. How embarrassing for Judas in front of the temple guard and the contingent who followed him. What was he to do? Where could Jesus be? Judas searched his memory and remembered that Jesus often went to pray in a garden on the Mount of Olives.

"And Judas, who betrayed Him, also knew the place; for Jesus often met there with His disciples. Then Judas, having received a detachment of troops, and officers from the chief priests and Pharisees, came there with lanterns, torches, and weapons" (John 18:2-3). *"Now Judas had given them a sign, saying, 'Whomever I kiss, He is the One; seize Him'. Immediately he went up to Jesus and said, 'Greetings, Rabbi!' and kissed Him."* Matthew 26:48-49

Peter tried to protect Jesus and cut off the ear of the high priest's servant, but Jesus rebuked Peter for his actions and asked the mob to send the others away. As the eleven disciples were afraid, they fled (Mark 14:50). *"And they led Him away to Annas first, for he was the father-in-law of Caiaphas who was high priest that year"* (John 18:13). *"Then Annas sent Him bound to Caiaphas the high priest."* John 18:24

While Judas is not named, he is still anticipating the 'Warrior King' to emerge. The apostle John, much later writing his gospel, remembered details the others weren't inspired to include in their accounts. Peter and John, with John's brother James, were the three close disciples who often accompanied Jesus on so many occasions. John remembered something that involved Peter.

"And Simon Peter followed Jesus, and so did another disciple. Now that disciple was known to the high priest, and went with Jesus into the courtyard of the high priest. But Peter stood at the door outside. Then the other disciple, who was known to the high priest, went out and spoke to her who kept the door, and brought Peter in." John 18:15-16

To substantiate the claim that *'that disciple was known to the high priest'*, one would remember Judas was the son of Simon the Pharisee. Jesus had previously said, *"Did I not choose you, the twelve, and one of you is a devil? He spoke of Judas Iscariot, the son of Simon"* (John 6:70-71a). *"Then one of the Pharisees asked Jesus to eat with him. And Jesus went to the*

Pharisee's house, and sat down to eat." "And Jesus said to Him, 'Simon, I have something to say to you'." Luke 7:36, 40a

Judas had previously met with the Pharisees and arranged to deliver Jesus to them. Judas, as Simon the Pharisees' son, could enter the Temple without question and was well known to them all.

Judas attended the first three trials of Jesus. First by Annas, the second by Caiaphas, and the third by the Sanhedrin, always waiting for Jesus to show His hand as the foretold 'Warrior King', the anticipated Messiah who would lead them out from under oppression and the rule of the Romans. But this did not happen, as the Sanhedrin found Jesus guilty of blasphemy and mistreated Him.

There is no more mention of Judas until Jesus is condemned and no 'Warrior King' had emerged, but an innocent Man.

"Then Judas, His betrayer,
seeing that He had been condemned,
was remorseful and brought back the thirty pieces of silver
to the chief priests and elders, saying,
'I have sinned by betraying innocent blood'.
And they said, 'What is that to us? You see to it!'

Judas the Betrayer.

Then he threw down the pieces of silver in the temple and departed, and went and hanged himself."
Matthew 27:3-5

The question to be asked is, "When did this hanging take place?" Did it occur at the same time the Sanhedrin convicted Jesus of Blasphemy? Or at the time when Jesus was handed over to be crucified by the Romans after Pilate washed his hands of the whole deal? Or was it at another time?

Comparing the four gospel accounts is required to give the full story of Jesus' burial. Matthew 27:57-61, Mark 15:42-47, Luke 23:50-56, and John 19:38-42. It was Joseph of Arimathea who claimed Jesus' body from Pilate, and along with Nicodemus, and the women who had followed Jesus from Galilee, hurriedly prepared the body and then left. The tomb was sealed by the Saturday morning. Matthew 27:65-66

Note. Joseph of Arimathea was a wealthy man, a member of the Sanhedrin and a secret supporter of Jesus, but he did not agree with the actions of the other members of the Sanhedrin (Luke 23:50-51). Nicodemus was a Pharisee and a secret follower of Jesus. He also did not agree with the decision made to have Jesus killed. John 19:39

As you read the above accounts, it was Mary Magdalene then the group of women who were the first to return to the tomb and found the stone rolled away. Luke's gospel was written later than Mark and Matthew as he had interviewed many eyewitnesses, whose accounts included many details that he discovered when interviewing those involved some time later. Luke added the following to give substance to the events that had occurred.

"Then they went in and did not find the body of the Lord Jesus. And it happened, as they were greatly perplexed about this, that behold, two men stood by them in shining garments. They said to them, 'Why do you seek the living among the dead? He is not here, but is risen! Remember how He spoke to you when He was still in Galilee, saying, 'The Son of Man must be delivered into the hands of sinful men, and be crucified, and the third day rise again'. And they remembered His words. Then they returned from the tomb and told all these things to the <u>eleven</u> and to all the rest." Luke 24:39

On the same day, the resurrected Jesus met with two people on the road to Emmaus and they invited Him to have a meal with them. One could imagine He sat opposite them both. As Jesus took the bread, blessed and broke it, there was no response until He offered the bread to them. When Jesus presented the bread to them, and they saw the nail print wounds in His wrists, their eyes were opened and He vanished out of their sight.

Judas the Betrayer.

"And they said to one another, 'Did not our heart burn within us while He talked with us on the road, and while He opened the Scriptures to us?' So they rose up that very hour and returned to Jerusalem, and found the <u>eleven</u> and those who were with them gathered together, saying, 'The Lord is risen indeed, and has appeared to Simon!' And they told about the things that had happened on the road, and how He was known to them in the breaking of bread." Luke 24:32-35.

There is a question that remains. 'Who are the eleven?' Did I hear someone say, "Well Judas is dead! He hung himself! So, there are only eleven left." Now let's not be hasty in making that assumption. We need to add more scripture verses.

"Now Thomas, called the Twin, one of the twelve, was not with them when Jesus came. The other disciples therefore said to him, 'We have seen the Lord'. So he said to them, 'Unless I see in His hands the print of the nails, and put my finger into the print of the nails, and put my hand into His side, I will not believe'. And after eight days His disciples were again inside, and Thomas with them. Jesus came, the doors being shut, and stood in the midst, and said, 'Peace to you!' Then He said to Thomas, 'Reach your finger here, and look at My hands; and reach your hand here, and put it into My side. Do not be unbelieving, but believing'. And Thomas answered and said to Him, 'My Lord and my God!' Jesus said to him, 'Thomas, because you have seen Me, you

have believed. Blessed are those who have not seen and yet have believed'." John 20:24-29

These verses shed a lot of light on the sequence of events surrounding the Gospel accounts of Jesus' crucifixion. It should be noted that Thomas was not present when Jesus appeared to the eleven. Thomas in this instance was the twelfth man. It would then appear that Judas was still around and had not yet hung himself.

It is difficult to state with confidence when Judas committed suicide. If Judas was present on all these occasions, I can't imagine the impact these visits of Jesus would have on him (John 20:30-31). Was Jesus' appearances the cause of his remorsefulness for what he had committed? We are not told.

What we are told is that the disciples went to Galilee to meet with Jesus (John 21:1-3), but only seven out of a possible twelve attended. While five are named including Thomas, two are not. Was one Judas? Did Judas see the restoration of Peter but not himself? We are not told that Judas was even in attendance.

There is still one more scripture that would shed some light on the death of Judas. Luke continued his account where the other Gospels finished, and supplied detailed information about Judas and his death and the cause of his death. I share the following verses from the book of Acts, which was written by Luke.

> "And in those days Peter stood up in the midst of the disciples (altogether the number of names was about a hundred and twenty), and said, 'Men and brethren, this Scripture had to be fulfilled, which the Holy Spirit spoke before by the mouth of David concerning Judas, who became a guide to those who arrested Jesus; for he was numbered with us and obtained a part in this ministry'." (Now this man purchased a field with the wages of iniquity; and falling headlong, he burst open in the middle and all his entrails gushed out. And it became known to all those dwelling in Jerusalem; so that field is called in their own language, Akel Dama, that is, Field of Blood.) "For it is written in the Book of Psalms: 'Let his dwelling place be desolate, and let no one live in it'; and, 'Let another take his office'." Acts 1:15-20

First, we know that Judas did not purchase the field but the chief priests as the returned money was the price paid for blood.

> "But the chief priests took the silver pieces and said,
> 'It is not lawful to put them in the treasury,
> because they are the price of blood'.
> And they consulted together
> and bought with them the potter's field,

> *to bury strangers in.*
> *Therefore that field has been called*
> *the 'Field of Blood' to this day."*
>
> Matthew 27:6-8

The second is the fact that Judas contracted a disease that made him swell up, so a wagon could pass where he could not. William Barclay in his book, "The Master's Men" has much more information about this subject. The disease that Judas was afflicted with, would have taken some time to manifest in his body, so one could imagine, this would not happen overnight or even in a couple of days.

A healthy man involved in the *'Passover'* meal, led the mob to the Mount of Olives and then attended three trials, would not have been seen as described. Much of the detail regarding his illness and the outcome is unknown, as well as the purchase of a field took time. The people of Jerusalem, including the disciples, eventually found out about the conspiracy between Judas and the religious leaders. Needless to say, Judas hanged himself out of remorse.

There is one more issue of fact that requires attention. Let us revisit what Matthew recorded previously about the actions of Judas after he had come to his senses.

Judas the Betrayer.

"Then Judas, His betrayer, seeing that He had been condemned, was remorseful and brought back the thirty pieces of silver to the chief priests and elders, saying, 'I have sinned by betraying innocent blood'. And they said, 'What is that to us? You see to it!' Then he threw down the pieces of silver in the temple and departed, and went and hanged himself."

Matthew 27:3-5

Matthew had wrapped up the final days of Judas into three verses. But what if we separated the verses with full stops? Four different parts would emerge.

- Judas saw Jesus was condemned.
- Judas became remorseful.
- Judas took back the thirty pieces of silver.
- Judas finally hung himself.

This would allow all that has been written to find its resting place in Judas's last days, not hours.

The chief priests and the elders would have attended each of the trials and would not be in the temple where Judas threw the money that he'd been paid, until after the nine days of the *'Feast of Unleavened Bread'* were completed. You would also be aware that at 6 pm the Sabbath day began, so they would all have returned to their homes.

Did Judas go through all the events surrounding the crucifixion, and finally come to the remorseful decision that he had everything wrong, and misunderstood what Jesus came to do? That he had betrayed an innocent Man? Then not being able to obtain any absolution for his sin, went out and hung himself because he would no longer be able to face any of the disciples or those in the Sanhedrin. What Matthew had written would now be in its correct place. But, we are not told.

When Judas committed the hanging is unclear. It would appear that he was present for some time after the resurrection of Jesus. It is quite likely that he confined himself to his home and hanged himself there because of depression from the outcome of the disease he had contracted.

One could imagine the stench of his rotting corpse would have drawn attention and when the hanging rope was cut, because of his size, he hit the ground and burst open. But we are not told.

It can be accepted from scripture, that Judas never received forgiveness for his sin as Jesus referred to Judas when He prayed for His disciples.

Judas the Betrayer.

"While I was with them in the world, I kept them in Your name.
Those whom You gave Me I have kept;
and none of them is lost except the son of perdition,
that the Scripture might be fulfilled"

John 17:12

And the Scripture to be fulfilled;

"Even My own familiar friend in whom I trusted,
who ate My bread,
has lifted up his heel against Me."

Psalm 41:9

Other books by the Author

Have you ever searched the four gospels to obtain the full account of Jesus life?

The Author, under their guidance of the Holy Spirit, took the words of the Apostle Paul to heart, when he wrote to Timothy and encouraged him to: "Study to show yourself approved unto God, a workman that needs not be ashamed, rightly dividing the word of truth".
2 Timothy 2:15.

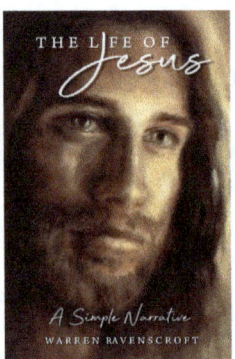

The Life of Jesus
A Simple Narrative

In 'The Life of Jesus. A Simple Narrative', the author used language, similar to the New King James Version of the Bible to order and blend the four gospels into one complete story.

The Life of Christ
Simply Told

In the Second book, 'The Life of Christ Simply Told', the author used language, similar to the New International Version of the Bible to order and blend the four gospels into the complete story of Jesus life.

Books available from
www.wittonbooks.com

Other books by the Author

The Christmas Story Retold

After attending a pre-Christmas church evening, I came away feeling numb due to the presentation of the Christmas story, by very secular people.

As you read, my prayer is that the Holy Spirit will not only impart wisdom, but a deep understanding of the real Nativity story.

**Books available from
www.wittonbooks.com**

God, Man, Lucifer and the End Time

The book contains a collection of seven stand-alone documents. However, they all overlap and combine in a way only the Holy Spirit could implement. They are complex topics, requiring a great deal of study to 'bring it together'.

Prompted by the Holy Spirit and this work used as the 'foundation', may it lead to a greater understanding of the truth, majesty and love of our God.

Books available from
www.wittonbooks.com

Other books by the Author

Life's a Journey

Life's a Journey introduces the reader to the road taken by several Bible characters and the consequences of their chosen walks. Those introduced are Mary, John the Baptist, Andrew, John the Disciple, and the children of Israel.

A second section brings a light-hearted twist, as the author shares real-life incidents, although the setting has been changed to add further humour to the already hilarious accounts of his eventful life.

Each of us has a journey to walk. Some long, some short, and some heartbreaking, others blessed. May each who reads glean encouragement for your life's walk.

Books available from
www.wittonbooks.com

Series titles available:

Book One	*The Defiant Mouse*
Book Two	*The Curious Chicken*
Book Three	*A Dog in Need*
Book Four	*An Old Friend Found*
Book Five	*The Rescue*
Book Six	*The Bush Fire*
Book Seven	*A Bad Influence*
Book Eight	*A Shining Light*
Book Nine	*Hidden Secrets*
Book Ten	*A Foiled Plot*
Book Eleven	*Running the Race*
Book Twelve	*An Unexpected Reward*
Book Thirteen	*Max Meets a Friend*
Book Fourteen	*Reflections*

Books available from *The Adventures of Max* Facebook page, and www.wittonbooks.com

Other books by the Author

Series titles available:

Book One	*The Servant Mouse*
Book Two	*A Cherished Place*
Book Three	*Manuel and the Spider*
Book Four	*A Generous Giver*
Book Five	*Lost and Found*
Book Six	*Manuel's Day Out*
Book Seven	*Love One Another*
Book Eight	*Observations*

Books available from *Manuel's Missions* Facebook page, and www.wittonbooks.com

www.ingramcontent.com/pod-product-compliance
Lightning Source LLC
Chambersburg PA
CBHW051418290426
44109CB00016B/1353